D1198781

WHEN LOVE IS NOT ENOUGH

When Love Is Not Enough

HOW MENTAL HEALTH PROFESSIONALS CAN HELP SPECIAL-NEEDS ADOPTIVE FAMILIES

Marian Sandmaier
and
Family Service of Burlington County
Mt. Holly, NJ

CHILD WELFARE LEAGUE OF AMERICA
WASHINGTON, DC

Sponsored by the United States Department of Health and Human Services, Office of Human Development, Administration for Children, Youth, and Families, Children's Bureau, through grant number 90-CO-0288.

CHILD WELFARE LEAGUE OF AMERICA, INC.
440 First Street, NW, Suite 310
Washington, DC 20001-2085
(202)638-2952

Current Printing (last digit)
10 9 8 7 6 5 4 3 2 1

Cover design by Anita Crouch
Text design by Eve Malakoff-Klein

ISBN # 0-87868-346-1

Contents

PREFACE

Family Service of Burlington County is a private, nonprofit mental health agency in New Jersey. Since 1983, Family Service has provided counseling and therapy services to families and children during and after the adoption process. This book grew out of its wish to share with other clinical services the knowledge and skills gained in serving several hundred families.

The author, Marian Sandmaier, is a writer and consultant specializing in mental health issues. She is the author of *The Invisible Alcoholics: Women and Alcohol Abuse in America.*

Mary Wells, ACSW
Executive Director
Family Service of Burlington County, NJ

INTRODUCTION

After living with three different foster families, four-year-old Jenny was recently placed for adoption with Marilyn and Don Ridge. The Ridges, who decided to adopt shortly after discovering they were infertile, looked forward to Jenny's coming with enormous excitement. Now they feel bewildered, and frankly desperate. Within a few weeks of her arrival, Jenny metamorphosed from a quiet, sweet child into a pint-sized monster: she throws tantrums at the slightest provocation, refuses to obey, destroys family belongings at will, and withdraws into sullen silence when her parents try to reason with her. At the same time, Jenny becomes hysterical when the Ridges occasionally leave her with a babysitter; at such times she clings desperately to her parents and screams: "You can't *leave* me!" Marilyn, in particular, feels alternately furious, duped, and totally helpless to affect her new daughter's behavior. She wonders silently whether perhaps she wasn't cut out to be a parent after all.

Thirteen-year-old Donna was adopted by Jim and Suzanne Colton when she was three. Their first decade together passed in relative calm; during the last six months, however, the family has suffered a severe shock. Quite without warning, Donna has developed a keen interest in her "real" family: who they are, where they are living, and what physical and personality traits they have passed on to her. Her parents have firmly and repeatedly told her not to ask about her biological parents, believing that the less Donna learns about that poverty-stricken, alcoholic pair the better. At a deeper level, however, Donna's reawakened interest in her origins terrifies Jim and Suzanne; they feel pitted against a powerful shadow family in a contest of loyalty they fear they cannot win. But the more the Coltons protest or dismiss Donna's need to know about her past, the more stubborn and hostile she becomes. In recent weeks, she has refused to call her adoptive parents Mom or Dad and has begun threatening to run away to find "the only people who *really* understand me."

Marie DeAngelo, a single mother, adopted eight-year-old Gina from Colombia only three months ago. When she met the little girl for the first time at the airport, she was shocked to discover that Gina suffered medical problems she had not been advised about, including infected sores on her face and neck and a pronounced limp. Unprepared emotionally or financially for these difficulties, Marie has frequently felt overwhelmed; nonetheless, she has done her best to care for Gina and welcome her warmly into her home. But her new daughter is clearly miserable. She cries herself to sleep every night, eats little, and cringes fearfully when Marie tries to hug or kiss her. While Marie had hoped that Gina would become fast friends with her biological daughter, nine-year-old Terry, the two squabble constantly, and Gina isn't above scratching and biting when crossed. Terry, in fact, is fast developing problems of her own: her school work is falling off and she has become uncharacteristically irritable and moody. When Marie recently called her mother to pour out her frustrations about the adoption, the older woman responded: "You know, dear, you can always send her back."

These families in distress bear little resemblance to dominant cultural images of adoptive families. Adoptive families are typically viewed as happy families, comprised of a big-eyed, grateful orphan, a pair of loving, rescuing parents, and perhaps an enthusiastic sibling or two. It is popularly assumed that these strangers somehow fall in love at first sight, readily bond with one another, and instantly embark upon a satisfying and rewarding life together. Although this scenario is clearly an idealized one, most people have been at least somewhat influenced by prevailing adoption mythology. Although many mental health professionals recognize that some adopted children have been traumatized by past losses, for example, it is often assumed that such "chosen children" will have little difficulty integrating themselves into their new, nurturing families. It is also commonly assumed that while adoptive families may encounter their share of problems along the way, on average their difficulties will be no more serious than—and certainly no different from—those of biological families.

ADOPTION IS DIFFERENT

In many ways, of course, adoptive families are like most other families: they can love one another as deeply, bicker as ferociously, and become as enmeshed in their own particular sets of family dynamics as any biologically linked group of individuals. But in other important ways, adoptive families are unique. Adoption represents the union of a child with parents and siblings who are not related by birth, but rather joined together through a process of law. This apparently simple but crucial difference gives rise to a host of complex emotional issues and needs that must be unearthed and worked through if the child, parents, and siblings are to truly become a family.

Today, the kinds of difficulties faced by the Ridge, Colton, and DeAngelo families are not uncommon—nor do they necessarily indicate that the adoption is failing. But these families do need help. In working through the network of painful, emotionally charged issues involved in adoptive adjustment, many families need the services of mental health professionals who understand the unique aspects of adoptive family dynamics. Indeed, in one study of adoption satisfaction among 177 families, mental health counseling was cited by parents as the number one unmet service need following adoptive placement [Nelson 1985].

Helping adoptive families succeed is what this handbook is all about. Its purpose is to help mental health professionals work with families to prepare for adoption, to maximize adjustment after the adoption, and to prevent tragically needless disruptions. The book will emphasize the psychological issues particularly relevant to the adoption experience, and describe therapeutic approaches and tools that are most useful in working with adoptees and their families. While much of the material that follows is relevant to all adoptive families, the book's primary focus is on families of special-needs adoptees: older children, those with physical, emotional, or mental disabilities, members of ethnic or racial minorities, and sibling groups.

When Love Is Not Enough also may be useful to child welfare professionals who are interested in working with mental health clinicians to serve their clients' postplacement counseling needs. To that end, one chapter is devoted entirely to the establishment of an effective working partnership between caseworkers and clinicians—a crucial and often overlooked component of any plan to deliver mental health services to adoptive families.

THE CHANGING FACE OF ADOPTION

Adoption isn't what it used to be. Thirty years ago, the majority of adoptees were healthy, white babies, while their parents were typically young, white, established married couples. Criteria for acceptance by the agency were strict. But by the early 1970s, the adoption scene had begun to change dramatically. The supply of healthy white infants was rapidly declining, primarily due to the legalization of abortion and the growing trend for young single mothers to keep their babies. At the same time, child welfare advocates began to champion the cause of growing numbers of special-needs children in the foster care system. Previously considered difficult to place, many of these children had spent most of their lives in a succession of foster homes. Priorities began to shift: adoption workers began turning their energies to finding permanent, stable families for special-needs children. The new call to arms became "no child is unadoptable."

In an effort to place these children, the child welfare system began to develop more flexible standards for adoptive parenthood. Many agencies now began considering applicants who were single, divorced, relatively uneducated, low income, or disabled. Parents over the age of 40 were being considered for the first time, as well as two-career couples and parents who were already rearing large families. The emphasis shifted to the degree of commitment and experience parents could offer a special-needs child, not their ability to meet restrictive standards of traditional parenthood.

While these changes benefited adopted children and their parents enormously, they have simultaneously created new strains in adoptive family adjustment. Unlike children adopted as infants, many special-needs children are seasoned veterans of the foster care system. Those currently being placed for adoption have lived in an average of 2.3 foster homes [Kadushin 1970], and therefore must cope with painful separations and losses involving not only biological parents and siblings but several foster families as well. Past neglect and abuse, including sexual abuse, are not uncommon. Moreover, the stigma and secrecy that still surround adoption are a breeding ground for identity conflicts and confusion for many adoptees. Consequently, many special-needs children come into adoptive families with deep-seated emotional difficulties. Many studies show higher rates of personality, learning, and behavior problems among adopted children, especially those adopted after infancy [Brodzinsky 1987]. When these problems collide with the often emotionally explosive issues parents bring to the adoption, the pressure on the fragile new family may be more than it can withstand.

How many families are at potential risk? It is estimated that one in 50 Americans is adopted, and as many as 20% are directly and intimately linked to the experience of adoption as adoptees, adoptive parents, siblings, biological parents, spouses, grand-parents, and offspring [Kirk 1981]. Moreover, more than 140,000 children are newly adopted each year [National Committee for Adoption 1985]. Of these, 14,000 are believed to be special-needs adoptions. Clearly, not all adoptive families are in crisis and require mental health services. In fact, many adjust reasonably quickly and easily to adoptive family life, while others may require only relatively brief counseling to resolve problems in family functioning. However, a surprisingly large proportion of families may face major adjustment difficulties: the National Committee for Adoption [1985] estimates that fully 25% of adoptive adjustments are in some way "unsatisfactory."

Even more disturbing, some families are simply unable to cope with the emotional strains of adoptive placement, and, in desperation, return the child to the agency before the adoption is legalized. Currently, it is estimated that at least 10% of adoptive placements are disrupted; for special-needs children, the disruption rate may be substantially higher [Barth 1986]. Disruptions are tragic for everyone involved. Families commonly suffer intense and long-lasting feelings of failure, guilt, and grief; many liken the experience to a death in the family. The children meanwhile, learn once again that in some profound and inevitable way, they too have failed.

Why do families risk emotional upheaval to adopt special-needs children? While few experienced adoptive parents senti-mentalize the experience, they are quick to identify the rewards. Says one mother of seven special-needs adoptees: "I have the good feeling of knowing I laid myself out for kids who really needed it. My investment wasn't in the outcome, but in giving my kids chances for love and growth they otherwise never would have had." Adds a father of two older adopted sons: "Once you accept your children, with their own identities and their own pasts, you can begin enjoying them for who they are. And there are those surprising, incomparable moments when you know you've made a difference."

For families in need, mental health professionals have an unprecedented opportunity to help make that difference. Although child welfare workers have traditionally provided post-placement support to adoptive parents, many new adoptive families with special-needs children may need a more intensive type of intervention. According to Elizabeth Cole, Senior Fellow with the Child Welfare League of America, "the average public child welfare worker simply has not been trained to deal with the kinds of complex family situations we are now seeing with special-needs adoptions. This is the time for therapists to offer themselves as partners with the child welfare system to help families deal with some very tough issues. The need is tremendous."

And by and large, child welfare workers know it. A recent survey of 20 Massachusetts adoption agencies showed that the most pressing and oft-cited postplacement need was for qualified mental health professionals "who understand the special issues of adoption....This gap in postadoptive services was found to be a prevalent and serious one, threatening permanence for some adopted children" [Frey 1986]. The time has come to bridge that gap.

III

THE ISSUES

There is a wide range of key issues that confront adoptees, parents, and siblings and that influence the success of family adjustment. These issues are directly linked to the adoption experience, although not all will be adoption specific. It may reassure families, in fact, to know that some of the difficulties they face are simply normal developmental crises weathered by all types of families. At the same time, one must be aware that certain expected developmental phases—the adolescent search for identity, for example—may be substantially affected by the adoption factor.

SEPARATION, LOSS, AND ATTACHMENT: ISSUES FOR CHILDREN

All adopted children must deal with the experience of loss. Regardless of how loving and welcoming their adoptive parents may be, they cannot erase a wrenching fact of their children's lives: separation from the parents who gave them birth. Older adopted children commonly have endured not just one, but several traumatic losses: from biological parents, from siblings, and from one or more foster families. Often moves are made with little preparation or efforts to help the children grieve their profound loss. On the contrary, many adoptive parents unwittingly sabotage their child's necessary grieving process. Anxious to establish themselves as the child's "real" mother and father, many adoptive parents discourage their new son or daughter from talking about past families. Many parents also have an enormous emotional stake in believing that the child is as happy as they are about the adoption and therefore may particularly prohibit expressions of sadness about past separations.

The consequences of unresolved loss can be devastating to children's developing sense of self. If no one ever explains to them why their biological parents were unable to care for them, they will almost certainly conclude that they were abandoned because they were bad and unlovable. An eventual adoption, then, doesn't make these children feel chosen or cherished, but only rejected once again by current caretakers. Some children liken the placement process to slave trading: to them, "up for adoption" feels like "up for auction." Feelings of rage, depression, low self-esteem, and acute separation anxiety are children's common responses to unresolved losses.

Almost without exception, children burdened with such losses will have severe difficulty attaching to adoptive parents. Attachment, defined by Kennell [1976] as "an affectionate bond between two individuals that endures through space and time and serves to join them emotionally," is a key condition of successful adoptive adjustment; a family isn't truly a family without this kind of basic connection. But children cannot attach to new families without emotionally detaching from past families. Without an opportunity to fully vent their grief and rage and to understand why the separations had to occur, they will remain emotionally stuck to the people whom they have lost.

Furthermore, many children have learned that attachment can be downright dangerous. In their experience, attachment has again and again been followed by separation and pain. Until children learn that they are not intrinsically bad and thus doomed to rejection, they will not trust their new family to love and keep them. In their minds, it is better to keep a safe distance from new parents and siblings than to risk the abandonment associated with intimacy and caring.

LOSS AND ATTACHMENT: ISSUES FOR PARENTS

Infertility

Parents frequently come to adoption with losses as well. For those who adopt because they are infertile, the losses may be multiple and deeply felt: loss of flesh-and-blood children, loss of genetic continuity, loss of fertility and all that means for sexuality, and for women, loss of the pregnancy experience itself. Profound feelings of grief, bitterness, anger, and sexual inadequacy are common. Too often, however, couples rush to adopt a child to compensate for their losses before resolving these intense feelings—with disastrous consequences. These couples may secretly feel such children are second best and never fully commit themselves to them. If children are continually viewed as symbols of biological or sexual inadequacy, they may evoke outright hostility.

Further, in their quest to bury their grief about their infertility, these parents may all but deny the very existence of the adoption. They may declare the subject of biological parents and even the adoption itself off-limits to their children, thereby both denying their need to grieve and conveying that their adopted status is somehow shameful. Although this response is by no means limited to infertile couples, research indicates that infertile adoptive parents are more likely to maintain a "closed" posture about adoption [Feigelman and Silverman 1983]. The irony here is sharp: in their rush to become successful families, these parents often unknowingly prevent their children from doing the work necessary to truly join their family.

Loss of the Dream Child

Parents typically come to adoption with great expectations. Imbued with popular mythology about adoptees, most parents expect a sweet, winsome, reasonably well-behaved child whom they will enjoy enormously. They imagine picnics in the park, cozy bedtime stories, and a son or daughter who readily giggles, cavorts, and cuddles. The special-needs adopted child, however, often bears little resemblance to this longed-for dream child.

Disenchantment can set in quickly—often by the first meeting. Many adoptive parents have put in years of hard work and patient waiting for this moment, and look forward to a face-to-face meeting with their new child with enormous excitement. They expect the child will be as thrilled as they are about the impending placement. Instead, the child may stare at them blankly, make a hostile remark or burst into tears. Note Smith and Sherwen [1983]: "...the adoptive placement is initially not 'home' to the child past early infancy who must break previous attachments and adapt to strange surroundings....What often is a day of intense happiness for [the mother] may be remembered by the child as an occasion of anxiety, insecurity, and possibly even terror."

And typically, the situation deteriorates further before it improves. Due to traumatic past experiences, many special-needs adopted children exhibit withdrawn, aggressive or even destructive behavior that shocks and distresses new parents. Recalls one distraught mother: "The adoption worker said Cindy had no problems, [that she] had been in a lot of foster homes and loved to read. So I got my daughter Cindy, who has a lot of problems and hates to read....All the things that I didn't want I got—temper tantrums, lying, stealing" [Nelson 1985]. In the wake of such bitter disappointment, some parents may never fully commit themselves to the child, or may even consider withdrawing from the adoption. Studies show that unfulfilled expectations about the child are a key factor in adoption dissatisfaction and disruption [Barth 1986; Nelson 1985; Smith and Sherwen 1983].

Why are adoptive parents' expectations so often out of joint with reality? In large part, the problem stems from insufficient preparation of prospective parents by adoption agencies. Because most agencies have only recently begun to place large numbers of special-needs children, many have not yet instituted programs to educate applicants about the complex problems these children present. In some cases, agencies may simply lack complete information about a child; occasionally, an agency may fail to inform parents fully about a child's condition for fear the parents will change their minds about the adoption. Too, sometimes prospective parents are so eager to adopt that they fail to probe in detail about a child's background or they do not "hear" information that is painful or threatening. In any case, poor parent preparation is a widespread problem: Nelson [1985] reported that 60% of the parents she studied cited major unmet preparation needs, especially regarding the child's past experiences and current functioning.

ENTITLEMENT

Entitlement refers to the conviction that one has the right to be the child's parent. Without this sense of entitlement—the deeply-rooted feeling that this child is truly theirs—it can be difficult for parents to involve themselves emotionally with the child. Adoptive parents face a number of barriers to a sense of entitlement. In a way, the adoption process itself is a long-drawn-out challenge to entitlement, whereby prospective parents must prove to an outside institution that they are good enough to be a child's mother and father. Adoptive parents often

talk of the anxiety and powerlessness they feel during this period. Even after a child is placed with new parents, there is usually a six- to twelve-month trial period before the adoption is
legalized. It is a period many adoptive parents liken to being on
probation.

A sense of entitlement may be further undermined by the
absence of social symbols and customs to validate adoptive
parenthood. Unlike biological parents, adoptive mothers and
fathers rarely are treated to baby showers, participate in parent
preparation classes, or are offered parental leave when the child
arrives. Moreover, adoptive parents miss the pregnancy experience that gradually prepares both mother and father for the
coming of parenthood. On the contrary, the suddenness with
which an adoptive placement often occurs—frequently with
only a few days notice—leaves many parents with a brand new
family member and an uneasy question: How could this child
possibly be ours?

The pervasive sense of insecurity that stems from doubts
about entitlement may make adoptive parents feel deeply threatened by the existence of their children's biological parents and
other important people in the past. They may refuse to allow any
discussion of these competitors for the child's love, or may even
denigrate them and thereby undermine the child's self-esteem.
The potential for entitlement difficulties should especially be
considered if the family is involved in an open adoption that
allows for some degree of communication between adopted
children and their biological parents. Even though adoptive
parents may intellectually appreciate their child's need to maintain ties to biological parents, the arrangement may bring up
intense feelings of "impostorism" and fears of being relegated to
second-best status by their child.

ABUSE AND NEGLECT

Many—some experts say most—special-needs children are
victims of abuse and neglect. Indeed, battering, sexual abuse,
physical abuse, and emotional neglect are among the chief
reasons children are initially removed from their biological
families' homes. Moreover, abusive experiences often lead to
behavior problems that may make these children vulnerable to
further maltreatment from foster parents or other caretakers.

A history of abuse or neglect may severely threaten children's ability to attach to an adoptive family. Maltreated children profoundly distrust adults and are likely to repeatedly rebuff new parents' sincere offers of warmth and kindness. Many such children simply withdraw from all interaction and behave in a listless, passive fashion; others are openly hostile, aggressive, and impulsive, and seem to seek out punishment actively. Most also suffer low self-esteem (believing they must be bad children to have been so cruelly treated), have little capacity for pleasure, and present learning difficulties in school.

Since they typically view their maltreatment as justified punishment, abused and neglected children rarely volunteer information about their past suffering. This is particularly true of sexually abused children, some of whom also have learned to equate love with sex and may not consciously feel they were maltreated. Certain kinds of behavior, however, should alert professionals to the possibility of past sexual victimization: advanced sexual knowledge for the child's age; erotic play, storytelling, or drawing; extreme fear of being touched; promiscuous behavior in older children; or patently seductive behavior in children of any age.

An adopted child's seductiveness toward a parent or sibling can cause outright panic among family members. Although the child may be looking for the only form of nurturance he or she knows, the parents are likely to view the child's behavior as a profound threat to family stability. Without counseling to help them understand the emotional and behavioral consequences of sexual abuse, a family may declare the child incorrigible and prematurely disrupt the placement.

DEVELOPMENTAL DISABILITIES

Special-needs adoptive children include those with various kinds of developmental disabilities. According to Hughes and Rycus [1983], a developmental disability is "a condition or disorder, physical, cognitive or emotional in nature, that interferes with the normal process of a child's growth and development." Conditions and disorders included in this category are learning disabilities (see below), mental retardation, cerebral palsy, epilepsy, autism, speech and language disorders, spina bifida, hearing loss and deafness, visual disorders and blindness, orthopedic disorders, and congenital malformations.

Few families are truly prepared to care for a developmentally disabled child. Such daily activities as feeding, bathing, toileting, and transporting can be difficult and time-consuming tasks that disrupt normal family routines. Moreover, many children have multiple service needs—medical, rehabilitative, educational—that are often difficult to locate and coordinate. Exhaustion, resentment, financial drain, anxiety about the child's health, and jealously among family members who receive less time and attention are common responses to the placement of a developmentally disabled child.

These responses often occur even when the adoption agency has tried to prepare the family adequately for the enormous expenditures of energy and resources required for this type of adoption. As one mother succinctly put it: "It's one thing to nod your head when you're told about a disability—it's another to live with it, day in and day out." But in many instances, families are not fully informed about the nature or severity of a child's disability. Particularly in the case of international adoptions, adequate records are often not available, and inadequate information about a child's medical condition may be more the norm than the exception. The ensuing surprises can have devastating effects: Smith and Sherwen [1983] found that adoptive mothers who had a clear understanding before placement of a child's disability and what it entailed were most enthusiastic about the adoption. Those who were taken by surprise—and especially those who were misled—gave the most negative responses.

The difficulties involved in adopting a disabled child are often intensified by a lack of support from extended family and from the community. Not only are both child and family subject to the usual prejudiced attitudes abut disabled people, but since the adoption is voluntary, the prevailing responses may be: "You asked for it—you got it." Others may assume that the parents must be paragons of strength to have taken on such a responsibility in the first place and therefore need little support or respite.

Learning Disabilities

The term "learning disabilities" refers to a range of conditions that interfere with a child's ability to take in, process, or retain sensory information. Levine [1980] defines a learning disability as "impairment in one or more aspects of a broad range of functional areas comprising such processes as attention, memory, visual perception, receptive language, expressive language, motor output, and higher order conceptualization."

Special-needs adoptive children are at high risk for learning disabilities for a number of reasons. Although some learning problems have genetic determinants, many are believed to be caused by an unhealthy fetal environment, poor parent-infant attachment, unresolved emotional trauma, and frequent school moves, for example. Because learning disabilities are frequently undiagnosed or misdiagnosed, adoptive parents often misconstrue symptoms of learning problems—poor school work, chronic forgetfulness, frustration-triggered temper tantrums— as evidence that their child is merely "uncooperative" or "not very bright." When the children, in turn, internalize their parents' estimation, they are set up for a cycle of failure.

IDENTITY FORMATION

Identify formation is a complex and multifaceted developmental phenomenon. According to Erikson [1968], its components include a conscious sense of individual uniqueness, solidarity with a group's ideals, and an unconscious striving for continuity of experience. Building a strong sense of self is no easy task for most individuals; for adoptees, however, it poses special challenges.

Among other factors, identity is shaped by one's personal history. When one wonders: "Who am I?" an important part of the answer is rooted in the family one was born into and who they were: Irish or Hispanic, tall or short, middle-class or poor, temperamental or serene. Most people take such knowledge for granted; adoptees cannot. Most adoptees are missing critical pieces of family information and need to fill in the empty spaces to feel whole, regardless of their ties to their adoptive families. Anthony Brandt, writer and husband of an adoptee, writes eloquently of this primal need:

> These are the most powerful ties, the one to the people who gave us birth and share our blood, to the genetic line, and it hardly seems to matter how many years have passed, how many betrayals there may have been, how

much misery in the family; we remain connected, even against our wills....The great majority of [adoptees] want to know, often desperately, where they came from; who they are; which parent or grandparent had the red hair they inherited, or the blond; where they get their talent for music or gymnastics, or the lack of it. [Brandt 1984]

The problem for many adoptees, whether adopted as infants or as older children, is that their hunger for connection to their history collides sharply with their adoptive parents' need to deny their child's past. Because of their own unresolved losses or shaky sense of entitlement, these parents may explicitly or implicitly forbid all discussions of biological parents and offer little or no information about the circumstances of the child's separation from them. Where most people have a vivid and complex family drama to call upon in shaping their identities, the adopted child has a gaping void. In the words of Frisk [1964], "the genetic ego is replaced by a hereditary ghost."

Not only does this void offer adoptive children no solid basis on which to build a healthy identity, but their imaginations are likely to pick up where the facts leave off. They may decide their biological parents left them because they were too bad, ugly, or unlovable to keep; in any case, the secrecy in which their past is shrouded can only make them feel stigmatized and deviant. The lack of knowledge also may lead them to destructively compartmentalize their feelings for the two sets of parents, so that one set (either biological or adoptive) becomes impossibly loving and good, while the other is denounced as totally bad and worthless. Regardless of which parents are labeled good or evil, this splitting impedes the child's ability to develop an integrated identity based on acceptance of both biological and adoptive heritage.

If adoptive parents have declared the past off limits, they are likely to encounter particular trouble when adoptees reach adolescence. If teenagers must work through all the usual identity issues appropriate to adolescence while at the same time wrestling with unresolved issues about their heritage, their task is complicated enormously. Some adopted adolescents, lacking any sense of connectedness to their past, may feel they don't fit into appropriate social, school, or occupational roles, and retreat into delinquency or isolation.

RACIAL AND CULTURAL BARRIERS

A transracial or transcultural adoption refers to the placement of a child of one race or culture into a family of another race or culture. Although some families adopt native-born children of other races or cultures, the majority of transracial and transcultural adoptions involve children from Asia, Central America, and South America who are placed with white families. Foreign adoptions are increasing at a rapid pace: more than 8,300 took place in the United States in 1984, up from 5,707 just two years earlier [NCFA 1985].

For foreign-born children, the adoption experience may be especially traumatic. Not only have they lost parents, siblings, and perhaps other important people in their lives, but now they are losing their country and culture as well. From the moment they step off the plane, they are thrust into an alien world: the landscape is unrecognizable, the food tastes funny, the people look strange and speak a language they can't begin to understand. All that is familiar and comforting in life is suddenly, inexplicably, and permanently gone. And in the midst of such enormous personal loss and culture shock, they are expected to tackle the formidable task of joining a family of total strangers. Few are up to the challenge. For many foreign-born children, the adjustment period is long and difficult.

Parents confront their own share of adjustment problems. Adoption mythology has painted the overseas adoptee as an adorable, dark-eyed moppet waiting eagerly for rescue by a new family. Few parents are prepared for the reality: a child who may have severe medical problems or be ravaged by malnutrition, abuse, or neglect, a child who may exhibit shockingly unsocialized or troubled behavior. One mother of a recently adopted five-year-old South American girl made this diary entry:

> Maria...runs in front of cars. She opens our car door and tries to get out while the car is moving....She grabs matches and starts lighting up her shirt. Hits and bites Jason and takes his toys. Jason is slightly taller but no match for her aggressiveness. I feel desperate. Exhausted. Resentful, too, of not having more information before she came. The ophthalmologist says her vision in that eye is only half what it should be—damage from infection. Nothing can be done. [Smith and Sherwen 1983]

Whether transracial or transcultural adoptees are foreign-born or native, parents often try to help the child adjust to the new life by minimizing all racial and cultural differences. They make no effort to become involved in organizations—churches, neighborhood associations, adoption support groups—that would expose the children to others of their racial or ethnic background; they may even refuse to allow the children to discuss their heritage. Whether parents do this because they think it is best for the children or because they themselves are uncomfortable with difference, the denial of background can only leave children feeling isolated and confused. They know full well they are not Caucasian, but they are not allowed to feel truly Asian or Hispanic or Black, either. Cut off from a secure sense of belonging to a group with whom they can identify, each child wonders: Who am I?

BEHAVIORAL PROBLEMS

When a special-needs adoptive family contacts a mental health professional, the presenting complaint is apt to be "the kid's impossible behavior." Studies show that behavior problems are among the chief reasons for disrupted placements [Churchill 1979; Kagan and Reid 1986]. The behavior problems of special-needs children stem from a variety of causes, including unresolved separation and loss, abuse, neglect, identity conflicts, and some developmental disabilities. The following are among the most commonly seen behavior problems:

Withdrawal from Relationships

Children who distrust adults or who feel unworthy of adult attention may simply avoid interacting with them. To these children, friendliness is only a cruel facade. If they respond and allow themselves to care, they fear the adult will betray them through abuse or abandonment. For other children, withdrawn behavior may be a symptom of depression over an unresolved loss.

Social withdrawal can take different forms: some children scrupulously avoid eye contact and don't speak unless spoken to. When they do talk, it is often in monosyllables with little affect. Other children shun all physical contact: they may pull away or cringe when an adult tries to touch them. Some of these children may have been physically or sexually abused; others have simply learned that this is an effective way to keep adults at a distance. Regardless of the cause, this kind of behavior can be extremely difficult for adoptive parents to cope with. Many feel rejected and incompetent; in turn, they may protect themselves by emotionally distancing themselves from the children.

Aggressive Behavior

Aggressiveness may stem from a number of causes. Like withdrawn behavior, it can effectively keep adults at bay. If adults are punched, kicked, spat upon, or cursed every time they reach out to a child, they are likely to learn to keep their distance. For some children, aggressiveness may be a consequence of stored-up rage at biological parents or other caretakers who left them alone and vulnerable in the world. For those who grew up in an abusive household, aggressiveness and violence may have been the typical way to express anger. Too, some abused and neglected children behave aggressively to provoke a response from a parent; to them, an angry parent is better than no parent at all. Still other children may behave badly in the secret hope of being kicked out and returned to their biological parents or a former foster family.

Overcompetency

Some children don't appear to need parents. They insist on doing everything themselves, from getting ready for school to mending their own clothes to cooking their own meals. They are usually veterans of unstable families who learned early on that if they were going to be cared for, they would have to do it themselves. Other such parentified children may be the oldest members of sibling groups and are accustomed to making decisions and caring for younger brothers and sisters.

Although this behavior may initially seem commendable, overcompetency often reflects serious attachment problems and low self-esteem. It also can be distressing for adoptive parents who have greatly looked forward to nurturing their new son or daughter, and feel rebuffed and inadequate by the child's show of rigid independence. The therapist may need to give parents permission to act as mother and father to the child and teach them to nurture in ways that will encourage trust and not threaten the child's hard-won self-image as a good caretaker.

Separation Anxiety

Adoptive parents are bewildered when children who customarily behave coolly toward them will hysterically cry and beg them to stay when they leave the house for shopping or an evening out. When the parents return, the children may retaliate with hostile or withdrawn behavior for days afterward. This kind of intense separation anxiety stems from profound fear of abandonment. From the children's perspective, adults are capricious and undependable: since others have left them forever, why shouldn't the new parents follow suit? No matter how many times the mother and father return, they fear that the next separation may be the final one.

Because the clinging behavior often is very trying for parents, they eventually may react with irritation and a greater need for distance from the children. This response only makes the children more terrified and anxious, which may provoke still greater parental exasperation. As one frustrated mother put it: "I thought I got a seven-year-old—and what I got was a two-year-old baby."

Control Battles

Every parent confronts control issues with children, but the issue of control is likely to be particularly salient for special-needs adoptive children. Many parents complain that their children seem to be constantly testing them by willfully disobeying family rules: not picking up the bedroom, staying out later than allowed, not doing homework, refusing to go to bed on time. No sooner is a rule made than it is flouted, making parents feel at once angry and incompetent. It is important to help parents understand that underlying the children's need for control is their desperate conviction that they are totally powerless. Throughout their short lives they may have been victims of unpredictable and terrifying adult actions: neglect, abuse, abandonment, unplanned moves. Each time they have been thrust without their consent into a new family, they have been confronted with a brand new set of rules—some of which may contradict the expectations of a previous family. Through their provocative and frustrating behavior, they may well be trying to establish that they have some small measure of power in a chaotic, untrustworthy world.

Delayed Conscience Development

Few characteristics in children disturb parents as much as a perceived lack of conscience. The children may casually and repeatedly lie, steal, or hurt others; when caught, they may respond with indifference or cool denial. To many parents, this kind of child may seem deeply immoral or simply to have no heart.

Parents need to understand that these children aren't fundamentally bad; more likely, they never developed a healthy conscience because of attachment problems early in life. The foundation of healthy conscience development is attachment to a loving, responsive adult. When infants' basic needs are consistently met by parents or other caretakers, over time the children incorporate these parental values. Lacking stable, responsive adults in early life, however, children are unable to develop a secure attachment—or the conscience that follows from it.

LACK OF SOCIAL SUPPORT

Research points to the importance of social support in helping a family adjust to adoption [Barth 1986]. Ironically, however, adoptive families tend to receive substantially less support than nonadoptive families from their friends, extended family members, and the community at large. This is partly a function of the adoptive process itself: because a placement can always fall through at the last minute, many couples tell no one of their plans until the child actually comes into their home. Thus many adoptive parents miss out on some of the traditional supportive gestures most prospective parents enjoy: baby showers, reassurance and child care advice from experienced parents, and the whirlwind of congratulatory phone calls and gifts that attend a baby's homecoming. Adoptive couples often have a sense of going underground to create a family and feel deeply isolated from relatives and friends.

But the adoptive process does not explain the critical, condescending, and sometimes even hostile attitudes that many adoptive parents contend with once the child comes into the family. For all the romance and mythmaking that surrounds adoption, it is in fact a deeply stigmatized institution. The stigma has several sources, including negative attitudes about possible illegitimacy as well as widely held suspicions that "if his parents didn't want him, something must be wrong with him." But probably more basic to adoption's stigmatized status is what adoption researcher Kirk [1964] calls "fecundity values": our culture's deeply held conviction that biological parenting is superior to any other sort. Consider the well-worn axiom "blood is thicker than water"; consider also the tendency of most people— including many professionals—to refer to an adopted child's biological mother as his "real" mother. Does that make the adoptive mother an impostor? This sort of nonreflecting chauvinism may explain why some grandparents and other relatives may be slow to warm up to an adopted family member, and why adoptive parents are subject to a barrage of insensitive remarks from friends and strangers alike. In his study of more than 1,500 adoptive parents, Kirk [1964] discovered that the majority had encountered the following kinds of comments: "Isn't it wonderful of you to have taken this child?" (92%); "This child looks so much like you he (she) could be your own" (92%); "He (she) is a darling baby, and after all, you never know for sure how even your own will turn out" (55%); and "How well you care for your child, just like a real mother" (22%).

The lack of support that many adoptive families encounter is likely to be intensified when the adoptee is a special-needs child. Parents who confront behavioral difficulties with an older adopted child may be told by family and friends, in effect, "Well, what did you expect?" In the case of disabled, transracial, or transcultural adoptees, there may be discriminatory attitudes to cope with as well. One study of black children adopted by white families showed that only 52% of grandparents and 43% of other relatives responded positively to the adoption [Feigelman and Silverman 1983]. Such "different" children may also face painful prejudice and rejection from other children, school personnel, and the community at large.

Single adoptive parents may need social support more than any other parent group, yet often have the most trouble obtaining it. Although research shows that adopted children of single parents adjust as successfully as those with two parents [Churchill 1979], singles are considered less-than-ideal families by many adoption agencies. Consequently, many are offered children with physical, mental, or emotional disabilities. Without a spouse to share either the daily tasks or the expenses involved in raising such children, single parents are often stretched thin by their commitments. Rather than offering help, friends and relatives often consider a single person's decision to adopt irresponsible or embarrassing and withhold badly needed support. Support does make a difference: one study showed that 72% of single parents whose close friends responded positively to the adoption felt that their child was well adjusted, compared to only 46% among those whose friends responded with indifference, mixed feelings, or hostility [Feigelman and Silverman 1983].

Many parents try to cope with feelings of isolation and rejection with a plucky "we don't need anybody" stance. Underlying such apparent stoicism, however, is often a deep sense of alienation and marginality that can undermine their sense of entitlement to the child as well as their overall satisfaction with the adoption. Some may try to bury their feelings of deviance or inferiority by denying that there are any real differences between adoptive and biological parenting. When this leads to "family secrets" about the child's adoption and past history, adoptive adjustment is in jeopardy for everyone.

IMPACT ON SIBLINGS

When adoptive children first enter a family, the children already there may welcome them enthusiastically. From their point of view, they have just acquired an instant playmate, a potential confidant, a new family member to show off to friends, neighbors, and schoolmates. But this initial burst of excitement often wears off quickly, especially if the adoptee is an older child with serious and demanding emotional problems. Jewett [1978] describes the changing family dynamics that contribute to disenchantment:

> These children may show remarkable compassion for their new brother or sister. Often they will go out of their way to help the other child to adjust to the family, mustering their own reserves of lovingness and generosity to share with the needful one. But instead of noticing what a fine job they are doing, their parents are liable to take their efforts and emotional strengths for granted. In the rush of constant problem solving that goes on around the new child, they sometimes expect

their other children to take care of themselves. Many times the "old" children begin to wonder if their parents like the new adopted child better, because he gets away with more things and the parents spend so much time paying attention to him.

Sibling rivalry is likely to be most intense between the adoptee and the child whose position in the family has just been usurped. If the family's youngest child suddenly becomes an older sibling, for example, he or she may feel particularly displaced in the parents' affections; no longer does the "baby" have all the special indulgences that may attend that position. The child may have to wrestle with birth-order power issues: Who is awarded certain privileges based on age? Who is accorded more responsibility? Who is assigned which chores? Who is allowed to boss whom? If the new adoptee has been inadequately nurtured, the other child also may grow to resent the stark absence of give-and-take in the relationship. Some children simply burn out from constantly sharing, helping, and mediating while receiving only increased demands in return.

If such conflicts are permitted to escalate without intervention, parents often find that they have several disturbed children on their hands instead of only one. In an angry bid to reclaim their share of attention, some siblings begin acting out at home or in school. Others become depressed and withdraw from family interaction. In turn, the adopted child senses the hostility of the other child or children, which only intensifies his or her own feelings of inadequacy and isolation. In light of the potentially disastrous consequences of such dynamics, it is disturbing that a recent national survey of 40 postlegal adoption services showed that family therapy for adoptive families usually included only the adoptee and parents—rarely siblings [Fales 1986].

IMPACT ON THE MARRIAGE

Some marriages are strengthened by the joint commitment of caring and energy necessary to make a special-needs adoption work. But for many couples, this pulling together process may be undermined by unresolved emotional issues. The infertile couple, who may rush to adopt before resolving their feelings about being unable to bear offspring, may encounter particular difficulties. If one spouse has residual resentment toward the other, deemed responsible for the infertility, the adopted child may only serve as a bitter reminder for both partners of the problem of the blamed spouse. Unresolved grief, guilt, and feelings of sexual inadequacy may further erode the marital relationship [Kraft 1980].

Marital problems sometimes emerge because one partner is more committed to the adoption than the other. The mother is often the more involved parent, perhaps because mothering is still more central to the identity of many women than fathering is to most men's identity. When one parent has acquiesced but without intense emotional involvement, the arrangement may work during the adoptive study and waiting period; but once the child actually enters the new family, this parental commitment gap can cause major difficulties. Resentment about the lack of involvement or support, or anger about demand for more participation, may make it difficult for parents to focus on the child's needs.

Further, the husband may feel outright jealous and resentful of the unruly little stranger who has come to dominate his wife's time and attention. While such odd-man-out feelings are common among new fathers, most men can better tolerate the needy, energy-consuming behavior of a tiny newborn than the aggressive and manipulative actions of an obnoxious eight-year-old. In some cases, the husband will pressure his wife to give up on the placement and return the child to the agency. Smith and Sherwen [1983] found that fully a quarter of the 64 adoptive mothers they sampled felt unsupported by their husbands and under considerable marital stress. Comments such as "At one point I felt I'd have to choose between my husband and son" were not uncommon.

Even when both spouses are deeply committed to the adoption, however, some degree of marital stress is all but inevitable. The day-to-day strain of coping with a special-needs child's psychological and behavioral difficulties may simply exhaust both partners' physical and emotional resources, leaving little energy for the marital relationship. These couples badly need respite from chronic crisis parenting as well as ongoing support from all available sources: sympathetic family and friends, community services, and adoptive parent networks.

IV

HELPING THE ADOPTIVE FAMILY

MYTHS AND MISCONCEPTIONS

While the adjustment problems of many adoptive families are complex and distressing, a knowledgeable mental health professional can do much to help family members identify and work through conflicts that are interfering with successful family building. For the therapist, however, a sure grasp of adoption-related dynamics is not enough. Underlying attitudes and assumptions about adoptive families can make the difference between an effective intervention and one that never gets off the ground. Most mental health clinicians have absorbed—at least to a degree—our culture's myths and prejudices about adoption in general, and special-needs adoption in particular. The following misconceptions among professionals are common:

"This is a pathological family."

Some therapists may look upon a special-needs adoptive family with doubt and suspicion. They take one look at the adoptee—perhaps physically disabled, perhaps a minority child, perhaps an older foster care veteran with severe emotional problems—and conclude that no healthily functioning family would choose to burden themselves with such a difficult child. Instead, they may speculate that the motivating factor is guilt, masochism, or perhaps a neurotic wish to be desperately needed. Although these motives may influence a small proportion of adopters, they are not the driving force behind most parents' desire to adopt. Nelson's study [1985] of special-needs adoptive parents showed that fully two-thirds of the parents named "attachment and attraction to the child" as their prime motivators. Fifty-one percent of the parents (some had more than one motivation) cited "availability" of a special-needs child as a key factor; that is, they were willing to accept the child because a healthy infant was not available. But while the adjustment process for these families was often difficult, few parents felt that they had settled for the child or in any way regretted their decision.

A family may also be prematurely assessed as pathological because of the level of dysfunction members display at the time of entering therapy. Chronic dysfunctional behavior should not be ruled out, but it is also possible that the therapist is seeing a reasonably healthy family in a state of crisis. Many adoptive parents, in fact, are experienced child-rearers who have had little trouble parenting previously adopted or biological children. It is only when the special-needs child arrives—bringing with him or her potentially explosive issues for parents, siblings, and adoptee alike—that many families first experience serious distress and disorientation.

"Many of these parents are ill-equipped to adopt in the first place."

Parents of special-needs adopted children are unlikely to fit the traditional stereotype of ideal adoptive parents: young, middle-class and married, with a stay-at-home mom and a successful breadwinner dad. And in fact, traditional concepts of what makes an adequate parent may initially seem to make many new adoptive parents appear unqualified to adopt: an older parent may lack a younger adult's energy; a low-income family may not be able to give an adoptee his or her own room or many material extras; a single parent cannot, in truth, be both mother and father to a child. Recent research indicates, however, that demographic variables, including age, race, marital status, maternal employment, socioeconomic status, and religion, have no bearing on the outcome of an adoptive placement [Nelson 1985]. Most experts believe that the factors that have the greatest bearing on adoptive family adjustment are personal qualities of parents, including a strong commitment to parenting, flexibility, experience, optimism, and sensitivity to children's needs. Parental attributes that may initially seem to be impediments may actually be advantageous to the adoptee. On one hand, a single childless woman may be a good choice for a child who needs very intense, focused nurturing or who has trouble tolerating triangular relationships. The child who is fearful of intimacy, on the other hand, may fit most comfortably into a large family that makes fewer emotional demands on individuals.

"This will be a quick fix."

Some families come into therapy obviously distraught; others may seem to function curiously well and appear to need only brief counseling to resolve minor family adjustment problems. Although the latter may be true in some cases, an initial insistence that "we're doing fine" may simply reflect a well-earned wariness of all social service professionals. Throughout the entire adoption application and placement process, adoptive parents have had to prove continually to various child welfare officials that they are indeed fit to adopt a child. Consequently, most prospective parents learn early on to present only their personal strengths and downplay any problems that might be evaluated negatively. Even in the confidential environment of a therapist's office, such a happy family facade can be hard to drop. At best, admitting to serious family difficulties may threaten the parents' own shaky sense of entitlement; at worst, it may activate profound fears of losing their new son or daughter.

One must realize, too, that adoption-related issues are unlikely to be resolved through any single therapeutic intervention. As the individuals and family move through their own life cycles, issues are likely to resurface in different forms and with differing degrees of intensity. Changes in the child's life that involve loss—moving to a new neighborhood, the death of a pet, school graduation, breaking up with a serious boyfriend or girlfriend—may reactivate the grief, rage, and helplessness associated with past losses.

Further, emerging concerns about identity during the child's adolescence may reawaken interest in biological roots, and both the adoptee and his or her parents may need further assistance in handling the feelings surrounding the child's symbolic or real search for the biological family. The developing sexuality of the adolescent also may pose a particular threat to infertile parents who have not yet resolved feelings of inadequacy related to their inability to conceive; in such a family, the pregnancy of an adopted adolescent may be exceedingly difficult for parents to cope with. It is important that mental health professionals prepare families for the reemergence of such issues and offer as-needed services and support following the completion of the initial course of therapy.

A FAMILY SYSTEMS PERSPECTIVE

There is no single best therapeutic approach to helping adoptive families. In most cases, mental health professionals can effectively use their customary approaches and modalities to work on adoption-related issues. However, most clinicians working in the adoption field believe it is crucial to integrate a family systems perspective into one's approach to understanding and working with adoptive families. According to family systems theory, a family is not a collection of isolated individuals, but rather a delicately balanced structure composed of interrelated parts. A shift in one part of the system, therefore, reverberates throughout. Satir [1967] likens the family to a mobile: if one changes the mobile structurally by adding or subtracting a piece, it is thrown into a state of imbalance that affects every other piece of the mobile. And so it is with families. When an adoptee enters a family, the position of each member shifts, often causing enormous stress. Daily living patterns may be upset, power balances may change, new alliances may be formed and old connections strained or broken. The job of the therapist is to help the family understand the sources of the imbalance, deal with the resultant stresses, and help each member find a new equilibrium.

Although some parents may come into therapy pointing their finger at the adoptee as the source of all difficulties, an exclusive focus on the child is likely only to exacerbate the family's problems. According to Berman and Bufferd [1986]: "The therapist who only works with the identified child risks creating a system that mirrors the cutoffs and secrecy in the adoption system. A child in individual therapy forms a confidential relationship with a therapist who, like the birth parent, will eventually disappear." Moreover, many parents may feel threatened by their child's one-on-one relationship with a therapist, who is likely to be a parental figure to the child.

Exclusion from therapy may also intensify parents' feelings of incompetence and helplessness, which in turn may deepen doubts about entitlement. The reality is that parents can be crucial resources for mental health professionals. Notes Jewett [1978]: "Parents are experts in how their family is not functioning—and their pain usually makes them very motivated clients. Listen to parents—their perception of the problem, what they've tried to do to fix it, and what has worked or not worked. Face it, they know a lot more about this family than you do."

This is not to suggest that a therapist should never work alone with an adoptee or with parents during the course of treatment, but only that an overall family focus is likely to be most fruitful. Parents seem to agree: in Smith and Sherwen's study [1983], the therapists who were evaluated most positively by adoptive mothers were those who worked with the family as a whole. Similarly, in a survey of 33 adoptive and foster families, therapeutic intervention was considered most successful when parents perceived support for the entire family [Reitnauer and Grabe 1985].

THERAPEUTIC GOALS

Each adoptive family is unique, and will come into therapy with its own mix of issues, conflicts, fears, and longings. Specific goals for treatment, therefore, will vary from family to family. What follows is not a blueprint for therapy but rather certain overarching treatment goals that most clinicians believe are important to consider in working with special-needs adoptive families. They do not address specific issues such as sexual abuse, behavior problems, or school-related difficulties, which will be identified as one assesses each individual family and plans appropriate strategies. Rather, the goals that follow offer an overall context for thinking about these families' concerns and needs and basic directions to consider in work with them.

Providing Validation and Support

By the time many adoptive families seek therapy, they have hit their emotional bottom. Parents, in particular, are likely to feel drained, demoralized, and inadequate, as the dream family they once envisioned has deteriorated into something akin to a waking nightmare. In many cases, past attempts to garner support have been met by misunderstanding or outright criticism from helpers of various kinds. When first met, therefore, family members are likely to exude a discouraging mix of hopelessness and distrust. They will not be able to marshal the energy or the confidence in the therapist to begin actively solving their problems until their most immediate and pressing needs—validation and support—are met.

Validation for what? First, for the depth of their pain. Many parents have tried too long to maintain the facade of stoic super parents as others have told them how saintly—or how strange—they are to have undertaken the adoption of a special-needs child. They need the therapist to understand and accept their wild tangle of feelings about the child they have tried so hard to welcome—feelings that may include rage, guilt, hurt, resentment, grief, and even outright dislike. They need recognition that they have taken on an enormously difficult task that would stretch any parents to their emotional limits.

At the same time, the family needs genuine support for their wish to keep this child. Relatively few adoptive parents come into therapy because their commitment is wavering and they want to figure out how to withdraw. On the contrary, most parents seek professional help because they have already tried everything they can think of to save their family, and they hope the therapist's guidance and expertise will give them a better chance.

Finally, and most important, family members need the therapist to validate their strengths: in short, all the reasons why they eventually can make it as an adoptive family. The fact is, it does require enormous energy and commitment to take on the adoption of a special-needs child. More than likely, the family has already poured tremendous reserves of patience, creativity, intelligence, and warmth into their efforts to make their new family work. Validating these strengths is not the same as promising that all difficulties will disappear, but the family does need recognition and support for their efforts thus far—and encouragement to look beyond their "failures" to the possibilities for building a successful adoptive family.

Working Through Grief and Anger

Because loss is a major aspect of the adoptive family experience, confronting and mourning losses are major therapeutic tasks. In particular, the adoptee must work through one or more wrenching separations: from biological parents, from siblings, and from one or more foster families. In many cases, the child has kept internal feelings about these losses locked inside for fear they will be unacceptable to the new parents and precipitate yet one more abandonment. The child will need to know that he or she will not be punished or rejected for directly expressing these feelings, and will also need help in connecting those feelings with the losses he or she has suffered and tried so hard to forget.

Parents also will need help in coping with their child's feelings. Even in the most emotionally secure of families, helping a grieving child is painful and demanding work. It often requires dealing with frequent and prolonged crying sessions, withstanding unpredictable outbursts of rage, and becoming a target for blame even as one is trying to offer comfort and understanding. For the adoptive parent, the task may be rendered still more difficult by entitlement doubts and hard-to-relinquish fantasies about the happy child they envisioned for their family. It may help parents to explain that the very intensity of the child's grief signifies an ability to attach to others—and that this admittedly arduous process is necessary to free the child to eventually attach to them.

Parents, too, need to grieve losses. These may include loss of the possibility of biological children for infertile couples, loss of an actual child for bereaved parents, loss of the dream child for those who came unprepared for the challenges of raising a special-needs adoptee. Any of these losses may be difficult for parents to acknowledge openly, not only because of the pain it causes them, but because they may fear hurting other family members—especially the adoptee. It may be appropriate, therefore, to work through losses with parents in individual or couples' sessions. Also requiring attention are losses that siblings in the family may have sustained: loss of position in the family as the "baby" or only child, and for all siblings, loss of a substantial measure of treasured parental time and attention.

It is crucial to convey to family members that grief is never totally resolved, but will resurface in the face of new losses, anniversaries, and other events that bring up issues related to original separations and losses. Josephine Anderson, a therapist specializing in adoption issues, cautions:

> If one is not prepared for [the resurfacing of grief], the inappropriate and unhelpful responses of denial, bewilderment, betrayal and even fear can result....If, however, the goal of "grief work" is reconciliation, then there is acknowledgment that review and reworking will be part of the adoptive family's life together. For example, some accomplishment of the child can be a

poignant reminder of the loss of genetic tie. Instead of becoming added emotional baggage, such resurfacing of grief can offer new possibilities for reappraisal and reconciliation. [Anderson 1986]

Building Attachment

Attachment is a cornerstone of successful adoptive family adjustment. Without attachment, family members simply inhabit the same house without the basic emotional connection that makes life together satisfying and worth the tremendous effort involved. Yet building attachment between a special-needs adopted child and parents may require hard and sustained work. Numerous impediments may loom: unresolved losses for both child and parents, an ingrained distrust of caretakers and identity conflicts on the child's part, and entitlement doubts and unrealistic expectations on the part of parents. Each one of these issues will need to be confronted and worked through to clear the way for attachment to develop.

Yet with so many barriers to overcome, it may be difficult to know how to get the attachment-building process underway. Indeed, one of the challenges of working with special-needs adoptive families is that tensions among members may be so severe by the time they come into therapy that there is not even much apparent enthusiasm for attachment—only discouragement and grim exhaustion. According to John Bowlby, noted psychologist and researcher on attachment processes, the first order of business for attachment development is to get in motion a "positive interaction cycle." In plain terms, try to get the adoptee and other family members to have some fun with one another. Recommends Claudia Jewett: "Encourage parents to try to develop some mutual jokes with their child, some games that get them giggling together. I tell parents to stop worrying about what the neighbors or the relatives or the school thinks about the family, and to concentrate on enjoying your child. The job here is to get parents and child feeling about one another: 'You're lovable, and I'm glad we're together.' This is the connection that forms the basis for trust, the criteria for whether a relationship is going to be satisfying."

Other therapists believe that alongside efforts to resolve underlying conflicts that may be impeding attachment, adoptive families can also build emotional connections through conscious "claiming behaviors" that emphasize the child's membership in the family. For example, the family may give the child a new or additional middle name with special family significance, involve the child in visits with relatives, emphasize similarities between the child and other family members, and help the child understand special family sayings, stories, and jokes. Some of the therapeutic tools described below—in particular the adoption ritual—may also help to instill a sense of belonging and attachment.

Accepting Adoption

In his landmark study of adoption, *Shared Fate* [1964], Kirk found that the single most influential factor affecting adoptive family adjustment was what he called "acknowledgment of difference." He discovered that those who could readily accept that adoption was a different way of building a family—and were therefore able to discuss all aspects openly and empathetically with the child—were most likely to be satisfied with the adoption. Kirk eloquently suggested why this was so: "By admitting our children's genetic and constitutional heritage we admit also their ancestors. Without doing so we shut off a part of our children's lives, not only against them but against ourselves." Many clinicians and researchers in the adoption field have echoed Kirk's findings, including family therapist Ann Hartman [1984]:

> The major developmental task for the adoptive family is to integrate the adopted child into the family without repudiating the child's past or denying the existence and importance of the child's biological roots. The major developmental task of the adoptee is to create a firm and clear sense of self through the integration of the heritage, biological, social, and psychological, from two separate families.

Adoptees cannot complete this task, of course, until their parents genuinely accept that they are children born to others and that those others are, and always will be, vital to the adoptees' identity and self-esteem. Parents need to understand that their child's compelling interest in his or her biological parents in no way challenges their adequacy as adoptive parents, but rather reflects a universal desire to connect with one's heritage, as well as a legitimate need to make sense of a profoundly traumatic separation. Viewed from this perspective, even the full-fledged search for biological parents that a few adolescents undertake is less likely to be a repudiation of the adoption than a deeply felt quest for self-knowledge and connectedness to the past. Parents need to know, too, that a family policy of silence on the subject of the child's past won't make the issues disappear—they will only encourage the child to fantasize in possibly harmful and self-denigrating ways about his or her history.

The ironic reality, as Kirk demonstrated, is that an environment of acceptance and openness about adoption is likely to strengthen substantially the emotional connection between adoptee and parents rather than undermine it. The more parents can show genuine interest in their child's heritage and support the need to express a wide range of feelings about it, the more likely their child will come to trust and attach to them—and they to the child.

Therapeutic Tools

Following are several treatment tools that have been specifically developed to help individuals and families work through adoption-related issues. In some cases, a family's adoption caseworker may have already made use of one or more of these techniques, or may be planning to use them with the family. The therapist should be sure to discuss plans to use them with the caseworker beforehand to avoid duplication of efforts.

In addition to the adoption-specific techniques described below, clinicians have found a number of other therapeutic tools helpful in postplacement counseling, including behavioral management techniques, which are thoroughly described in *The Child in Placement: Common Behavioral Problems*, by Vera Fahlberg [1979] available from the National Special Needs Adoption Resource Center (see Chapter VIII's "Training Resources"). Other tools especially well suited to family therapy work include family sculpture, reframing, and paradoxical interventions, which are discussed in detail in *Working With Adoptive Families Beyond Placement*, by Ann Hartman [1984] (see Chapter VIII's "Readings for Professionals"). Hartman's book also explains the eco-map and the genogram, two of the tools briefly described below.

Life Book

The Life Book is a homemade book covering the adoptee's life from birth to present, written in the child's own words and accompanied by appropriate photographs and other memorabilia. The book tells the story of what has happened to the child, when and why, and how the child feels about his or her history. The purposes of the Life Book are several:

(1) It can help children begin to talk about their past and how they feel about various events, which can be especially helpful for children who have trouble verbalizing their experience or expressing feelings.

(2) By helping adoptees retrieve parts of their lives that they have lost or forgotten, the Life Book gives them access to their own history and a sense of continuity that can help them develop a healthy, integrated identity.

(3) Through reconstructing the milestones of children's lives, the therapist has the opportunity to help them correct erroneous views of their past relationships, which can help them understand that they did not cause and could not control most separations—and that such losses are not inevitable.

(4) As each separation is confronted through the compilation of the Life Book, children have an opportunity to express their feelings about their profound losses. Working through such long-suppressed feelings can help them move into attachment to their new family.

(5) By providing graphic evidence that they have been truly cared about by others, the Life Book can help children develop self-esteem and trust in others. The handcrafted book also gives them something that is uniquely theirs to turn to when they need encouragement or reassurance.

Ideally, a Life Book is prepared when children first enter foster care and is updated regularly as family changes occur. Unfortunately, many children still do not have such books when they are placed for adoption. When this is the case, the therapist can talk with the caseworker about who is the most appropriate person to help the child construct a Life Book. Be aware of the commitment involved: the development of the document will require several sessions with the child as well as additional time to locate information and memorabilia. However, if it is agreed that the therapist will undertake the Life Book project, the caseworker will probably be able to provide considerable information on the child's background as well as leads to other information sources. It is worth noting, too, that the Life Book can be a powerful and effective therapeutic tool that may make it worth the investment of time and energy.

When beginning work on the Life Book, the therapist should keep in mind that it is essentially a child-made book that should reflect its author. Depending on the child's preference, it can be made from a store-bought scrapbook or created from construction paper and yarn. Other useful materials include crayons or felt-tip pens, paste, scissors, and colored paper. Ideally, it should be written by children in their own hand, but if they are too young to write, the therapist can record their comments in their own language. Include, at a minimum, when and where the children were born; descriptions of biological parents and siblings; accounts of all moves; descriptions of all foster families, other caretakers, and social workers who have been important to the children; any major health problems; achievements the children take special pride in; and memorable vacations, holidays, and other celebrations. Make sure the narrative includes not only the facts, but also their situational and emotional contexts: why parents and other caretakers had to leave, what it felt like to move to each new family, what it is like to try to love more than one set of parents. Visual elements accompanying the text might include birth certificates; pictures of the child as a baby and growing up; pictures of biological parents and siblings; a genogram of the biological family if available; pictures of foster family members, friends, and beloved pets; any drawings that are meaningful to the child; award certificates for school or other achievements; and letters from important people in their lives. If it is possible to contact any of the child's former caretakers, they might be asked for funny or touching anecdotes that can be written up and pasted in.

Although some aspects of creating a Life Book sound like fun, do not expect every child to be initially enthusiastic about the project. Creating such a book requires confronting crushing separations and losses, with all of the feelings that attend them.

If children tell the therapist "I don't want to remember," the therapist might suggest that while some memories may be hard to deal with, there also may be many pleasant ones that they might enjoy looking back on. If the children are agreeable, the therapist might take the lead by telling them the story of some part of their life, while they merely listen until they feel safe enough to become actively involved. But their need to go at their own pace should be respected. If they resist severely, the project can be put aside temporarily until they seem to be ready to try again.

The Eco-Map

The eco-map is a visual representation of a family's relationship with the world. It offers both the family and the therapist a simple yet highly accurate tool for identifying sources of support, stimulation, and pleasure from the environment, as well as unmet needs and sources of stress and conflict. For the special-needs adoptive family, the eco-map makes clear both how sources of nurture and stress have changed since the recent placement, and also that many of the problems they face are not simply family failures but emerge from significant shifts in the environment. Perhaps most important, the eco-map is a powerful tool for change: in the words of family therapist Ann Hartman [1984], it "points to conflicts to be mediated, bridges to be built, and resources to be sought and mobilized."

The eco-map is a drawing that maps the major systems that comprise the family's world and the nature of the family's relationship with these various systems. Appendix A includes a sample eco-map which illustrates common components. To begin, draw a family tree of all members of the immediate household within a large circle in the middle of the page, including the names and ages of all individuals. Next, draw in the connections between the family and the different parts of the ecological environment. Finally, draw lines between the family and each system to indicate the nature of the connection between them. A solid line shows a strong connection, a broken line a tenuous one, a hatched line a stressful relationship. The direction of the flow of resources and energy may be indicated by drawing arrows along the connecting lines.

Upon studying a completed eco-map, a family can often see with startling clarity how dramatically their interactions with the external environment have changed since their new child joined them. Frequently, both parents and siblings discover that many important sources of nurture or interest—hobbies, sports, time with friends—have dwindled or disappeared because of increased time and energy directed toward the adoptee. Some families may find that support from extended family and friends also has diminished—just at a time when they need extra support and validation for their family-building efforts. Finally, some families may discover that increased demands from the environment—medical care for the adoptee, special education programs, larger financial commitments—may be putting considerable pressure on particular family members. Yet at the same time they see sources of stress, most families are able to identify certain environmental systems that continue to offer potential support, stimulation, or enjoyment.

Having organized this crucial information, the eco-map can be a springboard for positive action. With the help of the therapist, family members can discuss how to meet identified needs, such as more time to pursue long-standing interests, development of a better rapport with a particular extended family member, or a more equitable distribution of tasks within the family to relieve stress on overburdened individuals. Over time, the family can begin to view the environment as an important practical and emotional resource—not simply a wearying energy drain.

Genogram

A genogram is a picture of a family over time. It is an information-packed family tree of three or more generations that records not only names and relationships, but also major family events, roles, and communication patterns. The genogram stems from the concept that the identities and life choices of individuals are profoundly influenced by their families. As noted family therapist Murray Bowen [1978] expressed it: "When I see an individual, I never see him alone. I see the generations of his family standing behind him." Used as a postplacement counseling tool, the genogram can help family members perceive the underlying meaning of current interactions and suggest ways to change family relationships and expectations.

To construct a genogram, use one or more large, blank pieces of paper (The larger the family, the more room will be needed).

Using the completed genogram in Appendix B as a basic guide to structure, start by drawing a simple genealogical chart of the immediate family, with a male indicated by a square and a female by a circle. A married couple is indicated by a connecting line, and children are generally lined up left to right according to age. A divorce is shown by a broken line, while a family member who has died is shown with an X across the name. Once the immediate family has been charted, expand horizontally to show the current generation of siblings and cousins, and vertically to picture at least two additional generations through time. Because the chart quickly becomes crowded with relatives, it helps to draw a dotted line around the family members you are working with so they can quickly identify themselves as they study the genogram.

Now the real work begins: filling out the skeletal chart with the "meat" of the family's rich experience. Add the following important information:

> Names—Both first and middle, if possible. Names can unveil secret hopes, identifications, and favoritism. Who was named after which relative—and what expectations might be associated with that naming? What significance do middle names have in the family?

> Dates—Dates mark the movement of the family through time. Birth and death dates show when members joined the family, their longevity, and family losses. Losses, in particular, have important implications for adoptive families. Does the adoptee represent an attempt to replace a lost family member?

> Residences—Place of birth and other residences chart the movement of the family through space. Such information shows major moves and may point to periods of loss, dislocation, or positive change. Charting moves also may uncover much about the family's boundaries and attitudes about mobility. Is this a family that easily adapts to new surroundings and experiences—or not?

> Occupations—Jobs and career paths tell much about the interests, talents, successes, failures, and socioeconomic levels of various family members. Occupations can also reveal much about family values and expectations. If

most family members are white-collar professionals, how will they feel about a child who wants to become an auto mechanic?

Health—Facts about health status and causes of death can indicate how a family views illnesses and disabilities, as well as what resources they may—or may not—have to deal with them. If family members already have experience caring for a disabled relative, for example, they may be better prepared to cope with the demands involved in adopting a child with a mental or physical disability.

The family picture that emerges from the genogram can serve several functions. First, it can help to introduce the adopted child to the family, both by cutting through the confusion of who is linked to whom, and by showing the child that he or she is now an important member of that family. Also, by exposing long-hidden issues that may be interfering with current adoptive family adjustment, family members can begin examining inappropriate expectations or working through unfinished business with other relatives. The genogram also may reveal much about the attitudes of extended family members toward the adoption itself, which can pave the way for efforts to increase understanding and acceptance.

The Adoption Ritual

The adoption ritual is a formal ceremony that announces and celebrates a child's membership in the family. It is a powerful symbolic means of validating the adoption that can promote attachment and strengthen a sense of family for the adoptee, the adoptive family, and the extended family alike.

One of the difficulties adoptive families face is the stark absence of any of the traditional symbols, customs, or rituals that support and sanction the entry of children into a family. Often adoptees are placed with families with little preparation or notice, then several months later are abruptly transformed into full-fledged family members in a brief, hurried legal process. The lack of any personal ceremonial event to mark the adoption can make it difficult for both the children and the new families to emotionally absorb that they are truly united. A formal, publicly witnessed adoption ritual welcoming the child into the family can both deepen the adoptee's sense of belonging and enhance parents' sense of entitlement to their child. Further, such an affirming ritual can inspire a sense of connection to the child on the part of grandparents and other extended family members, which in turn helps the adoptive family feel further validated and supported.

While the concept of an adoption ritual is new to many families, most are delighted by the idea and are willing to invest considerable energy in its planning and execution. There is no right time to enact an adoption ritual: some families want to do it as soon as possible after placement to lend momentum to their family-building efforts, while others may want to wait until legalization to celebrate. Since there is no standard form for an adoption ritual, the family is free to reflect its own particular style and preferences. The content can vary considerably, but it is important that the event being celebrated—the child's membership in the family—be stated and its meaning expressed in a personal way by various family members. Each family member should have the opportunity to speak, including parents, siblings, grandparents, and other important relatives, and the adoptee if he or she is old enough. Others who might be invited to the ceremony include close friends, the adoption caseworker, former foster parents, and any biological relatives with whom contact has been maintained. If the therapist and the family are so inclined, he or she may want to attend as well. Following the formal ceremony, the family may want to have a reception or party to underscore the joyful nature of the occasion, as well as give well-wishers a chance to congratulate family members and welcome the adoptee into the family.

MOBILIZING SUPPORT SYSTEMS

It is the rare special-needs adoptive family who can go it alone. Most need a variety of support systems, from understanding relatives and peer self-help groups to special educational and medical services and possibly financial aid. Although the adoption caseworker is traditionally responsible for linking families with community services, he or she may not be aware of a given family's every need. This may be because some families are reluctant to admit to problems for fear the child will be taken from them, or because the adoption agency simply lacks an extensive social services referral system. In any case, many families do feel unsupported: in Nelson's study [1985] of 177 adoptive families, fully a third felt that postplacement services were inadequate, and the majority believed that the adoption agency did not encourage postadoption contact. If a family has any of the following unmet service needs, the therapist may be able to work with the family's caseworker to see that assistance is provided.

Social and Emotional Support

Ideally, every adoptive family would be surrounded by enthusiastic and eager-to-help relatives and friends. As noted earlier, however, many of the people closest to the adoptive family may be initially uncomfortable about the adoption, especially when the parent is single or the adoptee is from a different racial or cultural background. Grandparents, in particular, may need some time to get used to the new family constellation. This does not mean, however, that the family is necessarily without sources of immediate support. Through the use of such tools as the eco-map, the family may be helped to identify others in their social system—a neighbor, an uncle, a single friend who loves children—who may be willing to offer temporary respite from child care, friendship to the adoptee, or simply a willingness to listen to parental frustrations and help solve problems in moments of crisis. For single parents, access to social and emotional support is particularly vital.

Even if personal supports are unavailable, however, most adoptive families have access to an invaluable source of help—an adoptive parent group. Sponsored by many adoption agencies and often by parents themselves, adoptive parent groups can serve as a useful adjunct to therapy as well as a long-term source of support for the family. They are available in most major cities and in many smaller towns across the country, and can be located through the family's caseworker, a state adoption specialist, or the North American Council on Adoptable Children (see the various resource lists in Chapter VIII).

Parent groups vary enormously in their longevity, sophistication and orientation. Some operate entirely as leaderless support groups, meeting weekly or monthly to share experiences and encouragement in their common efforts to build adoptive families. Others offer respite services to emotionally exhausted families, informational newsletters, referral services, and parent workshops on such issues as telling the child about adoption, feelings about the biological family, identity issues for adolescents, and the special challenges involved in single-parent adoptions. Some groups are inclusive, while others concentrate on a particular group such as families of foreign-born or disabled adoptees. Many regularly sponsor picnics and other special events for entire families, which can help adoptees feel less isolated and different and give them the opportunity to develop their own supportive networks.

Practical Support

Depending on their child's special needs, parents may need a variety of other services—medical, rehabilitative, institutional, child care, educational, developmental, and financial. The family's caseworker may effectively link the family with all necessary services; if gaps exist, however, the therapist may want to alert the caseworker to unmet needs. Although identifying community services and referrals is not always the therapist's job, the emotional health of the clients is certainly affected by their ability to get the basic services they need. The therapist's input can be vital: if the therapist knows a physician who works especially well with a child's particular developmental disability, for example, he or she can ask the caseworker to make a referral and thereby relieve a major source of stress for the family.

One frequently neglected potential source of support is the child's school. School often is the arena where children's problems are played out most visibly—usually through disruptive behavior, learning difficulties, poor grades, and sometimes truancy. If teachers and school officials are unaware of children's backgrounds and current situations, they may handle the situation poorly, by inappropriate discipline or by stigmatization. Once made aware of the problems students face, however, school personnel may be able to channel them into special counseling, learning, or incentive programs, and individual teachers may make an effort to provide extra support. While parents should be encouraged to advocate energetically on the school front for their child, it may be appropriate for the therapist to meet at least once with school officials to discuss behavioral and/or learning problems and develop a school-based intervention plan.

AN OUNCE OF PREVENTION: PREPLACEMENT COUNSELING

Undoubtedly, most therapeutic work with adoptive families will focus on postplacement adjustment issues. Nevertheless, there may be opportunities to provide counseling before a child comes into a family. The more fully prepared a family is to accept and respond to the challenges posed by a special-needs adoption, the less likely the placement will be jeopardized. In her study of adoptive parent satisfaction, Nelson [1985] found that inadequate preparation for special-needs placement was a major predictor of adoption failure. Of adoptions ending in dissolution, she notes: "One of the hallmarks of these adoptions was the parents' apparent lack of preparation for an aspect of the child's behavior that they found intolerable."

In all likelihood, few families will seek a therapist specifically for preplacement counseling. However, if an individual or family who makes a decision to adopt is already in therapy, preparatory counseling can be integrated into the ongoing work with them. Those who come into therapy to resolve infertility issues or other family-related losses also may be thinking about adoption; if so, the therapist can explore with them the ramifications of such a choice. In addition, the therapist's availability as a preplacement counselor can be made known to adoption agencies, adoptive parent support groups, and attorneys involved in independent adoptions. Counseling may also be offered in conjunction with assessment services to help an agency more effectively connect parents with waiting children.

If the family has already been connected with a child, preplacement counseling will begin with a concerted information-gathering effort. Urge parents to obtain from the adoption agency the child's complete history, including early life experiences, any physical, mental, emotional, behavioral, or learning problems, and all moves. If the family has difficulty collecting this information, it may be necessary to explain the reasons for the request to the family's adoption worker. In fact, it is a good idea for the therapist to meet with the caseworker before counseling gets under way to discuss mutual goals and avoid duplication of services.

Compiling raw data about the child, of course, is only the first step. The real job will be to interpret the information in a way that allows family members to understand how the adoption will alter their lives. It will not be enough, for example, to tell them that the child is from a deprived background. The therapist will need to convey the consequences of that deprivation in concrete terms: it may mean that the child won't know how to eat at the table, that he or she will throw tantrums when a parent leaves the house, or that he or she will show no affection toward any family member for several months—or longer.

The therapist will also need to explore how the upcoming placement will affect existing family relationships. If one parent is more committed to the adoption than the other, for example, it is important that both spouses fully understand the ramifications of their differing levels of involvement. If other children in the house express fear that their particular places in the family will be usurped by the adoptee, the family can develop strategies in advance for minimizing their sense of displacement. Many therapists working in the adoption field recommend that family members participate in role-playing exercises or other experiential work so that their new knowledge is emotionally grounded rather than merely intellectually absorbed. These exercises give individuals the opportunity to experience not only being members of an adoptive family, but also of being the child who comes into that family—with all his or her fears, needs, and secret hopes for love and belonging.

Preplacement counseling, however, isn't simply a grim exercise in preparing for the worst. It can also be a means of helping families discover and build on their own strengths. As family members come to understand the basis for the child's behavioral and emotional difficulties, they can learn how to respond appropriately and cope with their own intense emotions. Among other exercises, family members might take turns acting out their most dreaded scenarios. For parents, these might include leaving the child with a babysitter, confronting dishonesty, or dealing with seductive behavior. For siblings, feared situations might include sharing a bedroom or treasured toys, competing for a parent's affection, or dealing with threatened or actual physical violence. As appropriate responses are practiced and every imaginable feeling is expressed and accepted, the family's sense of confidence and competence will grow until they no longer need to harbor fantasies of the perfect child. The real child—with all the rough and tender edges—is finally ready to be welcomed into the home.

Preplacement counseling sometimes can be supplemented with hands-on preparation for prospective parents. Some adoption agencies offer families the chance to become respite families for adoptive parents needing a weekend off. Others have developed a buddy system that allows prospective parents to spend some time with a family with a special-needs child similar to the one they want to adopt. In addition, many adoptive parent groups sponsor programs featuring seasoned parents who talk honestly of their own early expectations, adjustment difficulties, and successful solutions. If such programs are unavailable in an area, the client's adoption agency may be able to arrange a visit or phone call with an experienced adoptive parent who can talk honestly about life with a special-needs adopted child—with all of its unique challenges and rewards.

V

WORKING WITH CHILD WELFARE AGENCIES:
A PRIMER FOR MENTAL HEALTH PRACTITIONERS

Counseling an adoptive family involves more than a therapist and a willing group of family members. There is frequently a crucial third player: the child welfare agency that is legally responsible for the entire adoption process, from application and home study to placement and legalization. A network of three types of agencies is involved in adoption practice: public agencies, which may be organized on a county, regional, or state basis; private nonsectarian agencies; and private, religious-based agencies. Unless the family is adopting through independent channels, they are probably working through one of these organizations. Forming a working partnership with the client's agency—and particularly with the social worker assigned to them—is vital to the therapist's ability to provide mental health services effectively.

Why bother to establish such a linkage? First, the adoption agency is a crucial source of information for the therapist about the adoptee's background and current situation. The agency should have on file the child's complete history, including medical records, school reports, psychological evaluations, and a history of all previous families. Moreover, the agency is likely to have access to the multitude of community resources needed by many adoptive families, including various types of financial aid that may be available to pay for counseling services. But the single most important reason to work in partnership with the client's caseworker is to establish joint goals and strategies for helping the family make a successful adjustment. Although the therapist may be formally charged with providing mental health services, the adoption agency—represented by the caseworker— is legally responsible for the child until the adoption is legalized. For months and perhaps even years, the family has depended on its caseworker for approval, resources, informal counseling, and indeed, for the adoptive placement itself. If the caseworker and therapist have different ideas about what the family needs, their separate efforts are likely to collide and undermine one another—to the detriment of the people both are trying to assist.

Successful collaboration between therapist and caseworker requires a substantial investment of time and energy. At the outset, the therapist will want to meet with the caseworker for a thorough discussion of the family's primary issues and needs, progress to date, appropriate goals, and strategies for meeting agreed-upon objectives. It is also important to clarify each professional's roles and responsibilities. The therapist's job may be to provide mental health services and the caseworker's to provide overall support and resource linkages, but the lines of demarcation are not always clear. For example, if the adopted child has school conduct difficulties, which one will join the parents in discussing the behavior problem with school officials? If the child has not yet made a Life Book, who will assist him or her? If a child wants to stay in touch with a former foster parent, who decides whether this is a good idea? Obviously, not every possible scenario can be anticipated, or needs to be. What is necessary is a commitment to mutual cooperation and open communication so that as problems arise, they can be resolved in the family's best interest.

The commitment is easily spelled out on paper; putting it into practice may require considerable patience and skill. The success of this collaboration will depend, more than anything else, on the quality of mutual respect and trust between the therapist and caseworker. From the caseworker's point of view, the therapist may be an important service provider to the family—but for some workers a rather threatening one. Up to now, the caseworker has been the provider of emotional sustenance, crisis intervention services, and all-around support to the adoptive family. Now a therapist has arrived on the scene, an acknowledged mental health expert who in most instances has much more extensive training than the caseworker and more formal credentials. Understandably, some workers may have decidedly mixed feelings about the therapist's role and its effect on their role. Other workers, long overburdened with large caseloads, may warmly welcome clinical help.

Therapists' approach to their work can do much to ease these tensions. Just as caseworkers may need to reexamine their attitudes toward mental health clinicians, therapists may need to honestly confront their attitudes toward adoption workers and examine how those responses might affect a budding collaboration.

In building a collaborative relationship, it helps to keep in mind that workers in adoption practice often stay in it for many years. Much of what they know is hands-on knowledge gleaned from long experience with special-needs adoptive families. This day-to-day experience has given many workers a highly accurate and sensitive grasp of a particular family's situation. They may know, in a very immediate sense, how the stress of finding adequate medical care for a disabled child has undermined a family's ability to cope, or how an adoptee's intense longing for a former foster family may be interfering with his or her ability to attach to new parents and siblings. Many adoption workers are also highly adept at finding and coordinating a variety of hard-to-locate community resources needed by adoptive families. Since many special-needs adoptive families have relatively low incomes, the types of social and financial services they require may be particularly unfamiliar to clinicians accustomed to serving a primarily middle-class clientele. The family's caseworker should be regarded as a crucial information resource—and should be encouraged to view the therapist in the same way. The more mutual education that takes place between the therapist and the caseworker, the better the client families will be served.

VI

DEVELOPING POSTPLACEMENT COUNSELING PROGRAMS: A GUIDE FOR MENTAL HEALTH AGENCIES

As the need for postplacement services grows, more mental health agencies are developing special counseling programs for adoptive families. Some agencies are creating full-scale postplacement counseling programs with separate offices and staff, while others are integrating services into their existing operations. Although a separate program usually permits a larger client population and higher visibility in the community, an integrated program may be the best choice for an agency whose financial or planning resources are limited. For the agency interested in developing either type of program, the following are some key planning considerations.

FUNDING

A discrete postplacement counseling program clearly will require sizeable financial resources, but even an integrated program will need to raise some funds for marketing, staff training, and perhaps even additional staff. Although private foundations may supply some start-up funds, currently the best source of funding may be through public agencies. Due to the burgeoning interest in postplacement adoption services, program funds now may be available from county or state child welfare offices, depending upon how services are operated in a particular state. (This may be found out by calling the county child welfare office or state adoption specialist.) In addition, the federal government directly funds some postplacement programs. (To apply or to obtain further information, contact the U.S. Children's Bureau, Administration for Children, Youth, and Families, U.S. Department of Health and Human Services, P.O. Box 1182, Washington, DC 20012.)

In addition to directly applying for money, mental health agencies may consider advocating for increased funds for post-

53

placement counseling services in their state. At regular intervals, each state is required to submit a plan to the federal government showing how it will spend its federal block grant for social services. Prior to the presentation of the final state plan, interested community members can comment on proposed funding allocations, through either a public hearing or the submission of written comments. Contact the state department of social services or department of human resources to find out how and when interested persons can have input into the state plan. If possible, encourage adoptive parent groups, adoption agencies, and other interested parties to comment as well.

The other primary source of funding, of course, will be service fees. Some families may be able to pay for therapy through private health insurance, but many will require government-subsidized services. Through the Adoption Assistance and Child Welfare Act of 1980, the federal government provides states with matching funds to cover a range of social service and health costs for special-needs adoptive children. In addition, all children who are eligible for adoption assistance subsidies can receive Medicaid coverage as well [NCFA 1985]. Since each state runs its subsidy program a bit differently, contact the state adoption specialist to find out about eligibility requirements, the types of therapy services that are covered, and how payments are applied for and disbursed.

STAFFING AND TRAINING

An agency developing a new or separate postplacement counseling program will probably be hiring a new director and other staff members. Ideally, look for practitioners who already have some experience working with adoptive families. If they prove hard to find—and they may well be—at a minimum select therapists who have some familiarity with family systems theory and who have dealt with some of the issues relevant to many adoptive children and families, such as child abuse, infertility, and separation and loss issues. Experience with children and adults who have been uprooted, such as emigrés, may be relevant. In addition, a background in child development will help a clinician readily distinguish normal developmental issues from adoption-specific conflicts and crises. Seek out training opportunities (see Chapter VIII) to familiarize new staff mem-

staff members with adoptive family dynamics and treatment considerations.

If a postplacement counseling program is being incorporated into an existing operation, the staffing process may require a bit more ingenuity. Chances are that current staff members are already heavily committed and may be reluctant to increase an already bulging caseload. If the agency can afford to hire new staff members or at least a director, do so. If not, rather than attempting to involve an entire staff in bits and pieces of the new project, identify two or three clinicians whose skills and interests seem to dovetail best with the needs of a postplacement counseling program. Give one of these persons overall responsibility for the program. To develop both skills and a sense of ownership in the new venture, take advantage of all training opportunities.

ACCESSIBILITY

To be effective, any service must be accessible to the population it serves. Adoptive families—and especially those with special needs—may have somewhat different accessibility requirements than the general population. Consider the following factors:

Cost of Services

Because many special-needs adoptive families have low incomes or are shouldering large financial commitments, many will need subsidized services. Be sure a program is set up to accept adoption subsidy payments and Medicaid (see Funding, above). Sliding-scale payments also may help some families afford treatment.

Location

Because adoptive families are dispersed throughout the population, the program site should be as centrally located as possible, and accessible by public transportation. If there is an existing program with a number of sites, try to provide services in several or all of them. Ideally, home visits should be available to families who lack transportation and/or child care. In addition, because many special-needs adoptive children suffer some kind of physical disability, the facility should be accessible to disabled clients. If it is not feasible to install ramps and other

special equipment at the site, consider using another handi-
capped-accessible facility for families with a disabled member.

Hours

Because the entire family will probably be involved in treatment, it is important to have substantial evening hours available
so that employed parents can participate. Equally important, a
system will be needed to allow families to reach program staff
members on a 24-hour basis. Particularly in the initial postplacement phase, midnight emergencies—a child who has run away
or become physically violent, for example—are not as uncommon as one might imagine. Some programs provide around-the-
clock access through an answering service, while others use a
beeper system. In addition, be sure that all staff members know
how to reach other emergency services, such as local hospitals,
child protective services, and physicians responsible for pre-
scribing any medications clients may be taking.

Long-Term Availability

For many adoptive families, mental health counseling will
not be a one-time commitment. Because adoptive issues change
and reemerge at different points in the family life cycle, many
families will want further services following an initial course of
therapy. This need may arise three months after therapy has
been terminated—or five years afterward. This means that a
postplacement counseling program should not be conceived as
a one-year pilot project, but rather as a long-term service that
families can return to whenever new needs arise.

COORDINATION WITH CHILD WELFARE AGENCIES

Even with generous funding, a top-flight staff, and a care-
fully planned program, a postplacement counseling service cannot succeed without close and continuing collaboration with
child welfare agencies. While this is an important consideration
for the individual therapist, it is even more crucial for a program
whose only clients are adopted children and their families. The
child welfare agency is the link to vital information on every
child and family in the program, and a key source of referrals as
well.

Ideally, collaboration with child welfare agencies will operate on two levels: program to program, and individual staff member to staff member. At the program level, one way to develop credibility with adoption agencies responsible for clients is to propose a mutual inservice program, in which clinical staff members would make a presentation to the adoption agency on postplacement psychological issues and the usefulness of a family systems orientation, while the adoption agency, in turn, would present a workshop on the adoption process, the types of special-needs families they work with, and postplacement planning considerations.

Once the program begins working with clients from a particular adoption agency, regular communication between the two organizations is vital. At the individual staff member level, each therapist will need to develop joint goals and problem-solving methods with the adoption caseworker responsible for a particular client family. (For a detailed discussion of the role of this partnership and ways to encourage it, see Chapter V). At the program level, try to arrange frequent meetings between directors of both organizations as well as regular meetings among all key staff members to discuss overall objectives and practices and resolve any budding misunderstandings. Keep in mind that adoption workers and mental health clinicians are likely to view adoptive families from somewhat different perspectives, and the mutual education process will be a continuing one.

MARKETING

It is sometimes assumed that if a particular service is needed and worthy, it will naturally find its market. Not so. Every service needs to make itself comprehensible and credible before clients will come forward. Indeed, since postplacement adoption counseling is a relatively new and often poorly understood service, vigorous and well-focused marketing efforts are particularly crucial.

Where does one start? Cultivating professional referral sources is a logical place to begin. Contact the adoption specialist in the county or state department of social services and ask for a list of all licensed adoption agencies in the area. Call the director of each one and ask to make a presentation about the nature and scope of a new program, the agency's background and expertise, counseling fees, and how collaboration with the adoption agency is envisioned. The agency should make itself known as well to providers who are likely to come into contact with special-needs adoptive families, including pediatricians, school guidance counselors, directors of school programs for disabled and emotionally disturbed children, child abuse specialists, hospital mental health practitioners, and officials of adolescent drug and alcohol abuse programs. These contacts can be made through individual meetings or, more efficiently, by arranging to speak at local professional conferences and workshops.

In addition to establishing professional contacts, the agency can also go directly to the client: parents of adoptive children. The state or county adoption specialist can provide a list of adoptive parent groups in the area, including those with a particular focus on special-needs adoptions. Staff members can ask to speak to parent group meetings so that parents can meet them face-to-face and ask questions about the type, scope, and cost of the counseling provided. (Staff members also may learn quite a bit about special-needs adoption issues through such a meeting with experienced parents.) Do not underestimate these self-help groups as a source of referrals: according to a national survey of postlegal adoption services, the majority of parent groups maintained a "sophisticated referral system to therapists" [Fales 1986].

Adoptive parents can also be reached by speaking at the meetings of family-oriented community organizations, parent-teacher associations, and church groups. Other avenues of publicity include paid advertisements in local newspapers, radio public service announcements, and free listings of special workshops or presentations in some newspapers' weekly activity guides. If the community sponsors a social services information and referral helpline, be sure the new program is listed.

VII

A Different Kind of Success Story

Helping adoptive families requires much of mental health professionals: energy, perspective, imagination, and perhaps most important, the conviction that you can make a difference. Given the enormously complex challenges facing many of these families, you may well ask yourself: Is getting involved worth the effort? Can special-needs adoptive families really succeed?

While there is no shortage of statistics and expert opinion on the subject, the truth may depend, in large measure, on what is meant by success. If it means a relatively predictable and crisis-free family experience, then it probably can be said that few special-needs adoptive families succeed—with or without therapy. But if the definition of success can expand to encompass the process of learning to accept and love one's child for who he or she is, of reveling in small, shaky steps toward "familyness" as well as major breakthroughs, of finding deep satisfaction in giving a child a chance for intimacy and caring, then many—probably most—special-needs adoptive families are entirely capable of making it. Following is one single-parent adoptive father's very different kind of success story:

> When I got my first son, who was 12 at the time, I had fantastic expectations. I thought that by having a family and roots, he would change dramatically. You know, love will find a way. But he hasn't changed the way I'd dreamed. He's 18 now, and he's still in trouble. Still having serious problems.
>
> That sounds terrible, but it isn't. Because I've learned to love the person he is. I had manufactured a dream child, and I had to let go of the dream. I had to let go of the need to save him or remake him. It wasn't easy. But in that process, I got myself a son, and I could delight in who he really is. He's independent, bright, resourceful, charming, and he lets me into his life to the extent that he can.

This is a child who was expected to be in an institution throughout his adolescence. I gave him a chance for something better.

I got my second son when he was five. He had no language at all, and was severely learning disabled. My eyes were wide open by the time he came into the family, so it's been a bit easier. He's nine now, and he's made tremendous strides. When I watch him do simple things—ride his bike around the block, for instance—I feel amazing pride and joy. He's still not sure this family is forever, but I see the trust level slowly grow. Our sense of family has become stronger and stronger, and for me, my life is enriched. I wanted to be a parent, and I am a parent.

There is something else about these kids—a quality of survival. Both of my kids are survivors. After everything they'd been through, they were willing to take a risk with another family. When people tell me I have guts to take on two older adopted kids, I say, you want to see guts? Look at my kids.

VIII

RESOURCES

TRAINING RESOURCES

Family Service of Burlington County

Adoption Support Program
Woodlane Road
PO Box 588
Mount Holly, NJ 08060
(609) 267-5928
Resources include this handbook (*When Love Is Not Enough*) and training packages tailored to individual needs, such as:

Clinical Issues in Adoptive Families

Treating Sexually Abused Adoptive Children

Program Design for Postadoptive Services

Public-Private Cooperation in Postadoptive Services

Developing Mental Health Services for Adoptive Families

Illinois Department of Children and Family Services

100 W Randolph Street Suite 6-100
Chicago, IL 60601
(312) 917-6800
Resources include *After Adoption: A Manual for Professionals Working with Adoptive Families*, which includes chapters on the unique aspects of adoption, identifying difficulties, postadoptive diagnostic assessment, and intervention with adoptive families. Also available is a companion training guide for *After Adoption*.

Kentucky Department of Mental Health/Mental Retardation Services

Children and Youth Services
275 E Main Street
Frankfurt, KY 40621
(502) 564-7610
The following two-hour workshop modules are available for use with groups of adoptive parents:

The Adoptive Family—This workshop will address normal family interaction, interaction in an adoptive family, and ways for parents to take care of their own needs.

Helping Your Child Behave—This workshop will address discipline with emphasis on building a child's self-esteem. It will also include material about normal developmental stages and behavioral expectations for special-needs children.

Adolescent Issues—This workshop will address identity, the internal search, fulfilling a family myth, and normal adolescent tasks.

The Sexually Abused Child—This workshop will address normal sexual development as well as the "how tos" of living with a sexually abused child.

Attachment and Commitment—This two-workshop unit will address the complexities of the attachment and bonding process and will consider the adoption triangle of the child, the adoptive parents, and the biological parents. It will also address the ambivalent feelings of adoptive parents as well as their concerns about search issues.

Medina Children's Service

PO Box 22638
Seattle, WA 98122
(206) 324-9470
Available training modules include:

Therapy With Adoptive Families—A workshop for mental health professionals to sensitize them to the unique circumstances and dynamics of adoptive families, and offer suggestions for appropriate and effective interventions. (Contact Norma Nelson or Karin Williams at above address.)

Teaming Workers and Families—A workshop to teach adoption workers and adoptive parent volunteers to work together to prepare and support special needs adoptive families. (Contact Norma Nelson or Karin Williams at above address.)

Intervention Skills Building—A workshop designed to teach crisis intervention and family living skills that are particularly useful to adoptive families. (Contact Shelley Leavitt at Behavioral Science Institute, 1717 South 341st Place, Federal Way, WA (206) 927-1550.)

The Mental Health Association in Butler County

127 East Wayne Street
Butler, PA 16001
(412) 287-1965
Resources include:

Adoption Resources for Mental Health Professionals—A 321-page book of essays on issues and treatment considerations for special needs adoptive families, including chapters on grief issues, disruptions, transracial adoptions, identity formation, attachment problems, the special needs of sexually abused children, and prevention considerations. (Price: $20.00)

Focusing Training for Mental Health Professionals on Issues of Foster Care and Adoption—A 47-page manual that discusses the child's experience in the child welfare system, how families and therapists view each other, and treatment approaches and tools for use in working with adoptive families. (Price $6.00)

National Resource Center for Special Needs Adoption

A Division of Spaulding for Children
PO Box 337
Chelsea, MI 48118
(313) 475-8693

This center offers a wide variety of training workshops, consulting services, publications, and other resources on special needs adoptions. Workshops of particular interest to mental health professionals include:

Providing Postadoption Services—this workshop considers what constitutes postadoption services and why they are necessary. Three kinds of services are described: remedial services, crisis intervention, and ongoing support services. The duration of postadoption services, the source of services, and the funding of services also are examined.

Understanding Disruption—This workshop examines disruption through careful definition, exploration of the origins of disruption, and step-by-step analysis of the pattern of disruption. Strategies for earliest possible intervention are offered. A distinction is drawn between "disruption" and "dissolution" (an adoption which is rescinded after legal completion) and current research is reviewed for practice implications.

Working With Black Families—New adoption approaches for working with the black child, particularly the older child, are described. Family techniques and the involvement of extended family are emphasized along with ethnic-sensitive practices.

University of Southern Maine

Center for Research and Advanced Study
246 Deering Avenue
Portland, ME 04102
(207) 780-4430

The following training resources focus on older adopted children and their families:

Videotape—This tape explores mental health issues and approaches relevant to older adopted children and their families. Experienced mental health professionals speak about their work and adoptive families describe their experiences and the services from which they have benefited.

Curriculum—This training tool provides information about postadoption issues for older adopted children and their families and models of mental health and other support services designed for this population. Trainees will learn about a variety of approaches through use of lecture, participation in small groups and utilization of case examples. Information and experiences will enable the trainee to identify personal and agency goals for program development, future training and the need for referral sources.

Handbook—This handbook will provide detailed information about clinical, educational and social programs for older adopted children and their families and the administrative structures needed to support the development and implementation of these services.

NATIONAL ORGANIZATIONS

American Adoption Congress

PO Box 44040
L'Enfant Plaza Station
Washington, DC 20026-0040
(505) 296-2198 (New Mexico)
The AAC's purposes are to further by study, research, teaching, and conferences, information on adoption and related social-psychological issues. It also acts as a national clearinghouse and public information center, publishes bibliographies, and operates a speaker's bureau.

Child Welfare League of America

440 First Street, NW, Suite 310
Washington, DC 20001
(202) 638-2952
CWLA is a membership organization devoted to the improvement of care and services for deprived, dependent, or neglected children, youth and their families. It provides consultation, conducts research and maintains a large library and information service. It offers a number of publications on postplacement needs, including *Working With Adoptive Families Be-*

yond Placement, Post-Legal Adoption Services Today, and several relating to adolescence.

National Committee for Adoption

2025 M Street NW Suite 512
Washington, DC 20036
(202) 463-7559

This group serves as an information clearinghouse. It publishes periodicals, an annotated bibliography, a list of books available through its bookstore, and Adoption Factbook, which provides current statistics about United States adoption. The NCFA also maintains a speakers' bureau and provides consultation services.

North American Council on Adoptable Children

1821 University Avenue
Suite 275 South
Grieggs-Midway Building
St. Paul, MN 55101
(612) 644-3036

The NACAC is composed primarily of adoptive parents of special-needs children and others concerned with each child's right to a permanent, loving home. Lists of adoptive parent support groups are available at no cost. Other publications include parent preparation handbooks and a quarterly newsletter, Adoptalk. The organization sponsors an annual training conference and provides financial and technical assistance to parent groups.

STATE ADOPTION SPECIALISTS

State adoption specialists may be able to provide information on laws and regulations affecting adoption as well as lists of licensed adoption agencies, adoptive parent groups and search organizations in each state. A complete listing by state begins on the following page.

Ms. Emogene Austin
Alabama Department of Pensions
    and Security
64 North Union Street
Montgomery, Alabama 36130
(205) 261-3190

Ms. Martha Holmberg
Alaska Department of Health and
    Social Services
Pouch H-05
Juneau, Alaska 99811
(907) 465-3631

Princess Lucas Wilson
Arizona Department of Economic
    Security
1400 West Washington, 940A
Phoenix, Arizona 85007
(602) 255-3981

Ms. Carol Wilson
Arkansas Department of Human
    Services
PO Box 1437
Little Rock, Arkansas 72203
(501) 371-2207

Mr. James Brown
California Department of Social
    Services
744 P Street, M/S. 19-31
Sacramento, California 95814
(916) 445-3146

Ms. Barbara Kilmore
Colorado Department of Social
    Services
PO Box 181000
Denver, Colorado 80218-0899
(303) 294-2859

Mr. Dale Maynard
Connecticut Department of Children
    and Youth Services
176 Sigourney Street
Hartford, Connecticut 06105
(203) 566-7303

Ms. Carol King
~ ·   · ~----•----+ -€ Children.

1824 Market Street
Wilmington, Delaware 19801
(302) 571-6419

Ms. Evelyn Andrews
District of Columbia
Department of Human Services
500 First Street, NW/8th Floor
Washington, DC 20001
(202) 724-2093

Ms. Gloria Walker
Florida Department of Health and
    Rehabilitative Services
1317 Winewood, Building 8
Tallahassee, Florida 32301
(904) 488-8000

(To Be Appointed)
Georgia Department of Human
    Resources
787 Peachtree Street NE
Atlanta, Georgia 30309
(404) 894-3376

Ms. Beatrice Yuh
Hawaii Department of Social Services
    and Housing
PO Box 339
Honolulu, Hawaii 96809
(808) 548-6739

Ms. Shirley Wheatley
Idaho Department of Health and
    Welfare
Statehouse
Boise, Idaho 83720
(208) 384-3546

Mr. Gary Morgan
Illinois Department of Children and
    Family Services
100 West Randolph
Chicago, Illinois 60612
(312) 917-6864

Ms. Pat Vesper
Indiana Department of Public
    Welfare
Child Welfare and Social Services
141 South Meridian Street

Ms. Margaret Corkery
Iowa Department of Human Services
Hoover State Office Building
Des Moines, Iowa 50319
(515) 281-6216

Ms. Barbara Stodgell
Kansas Department of Social and
    Rehabilitation Services
2700 West 6th Street
Topeka, Kansas 66606
(913) 296-4661

Ms. Sue Howard
Kentucky Cabinet for Human
    Resources
275 East Main Street, 6th Floor West
Frankfort, Kentucky 40621
(502) 564-2136

Ms. Nancy Miller
Louisiana Department of Health and
    Human Resources
Division of Youth and Families
PO Box 3318
Baton Rouge, Louisiana 70821
(504) 342-4028

Ms. Leanore Taylor
Maine Department of Human
    Services
State House, 221 State Street
Augusta, Maine 04333
(207) 289-2971

Ms. Fern Blake
Social Services Administration
300 West Preston Street
Baltimore, Maryland 21201
(301) 576-3258

Ms. Linda Spears
Massachusetts Department of Social
    Services
150 Causeway Street
Boston, Massachusetts 02114
(617) 727-0900 (extension 231)

Mr. Richard Hoekstra
Michigan Department of Social
    Services

PO Box 30037
Lansing, Michigan 48909
(517) 373-4021

Ms. Ruth Weidell
Minnesota Department of Human
    Services
Centennial Office Building
St. Paul, Minnesota 55155
(612) 296-3740

Ms. Mary Ann Everett
Mississippi Department of Public
    Welfare
PO Box 352
Jacksonville, Mississippi 39205
(601) 354-0341

Mr. Fred Simmons
Missouri Department of Social
    Services
PO Box 88
Jefferson City, Missouri 65103
(314) 751-4832

Ms. Betty Bay
Montana Department of Social and
    Rehabilitative Services
PO Box 4210
Helena, Montana 59604
(406) 444-3865

Ms. Margaret Bitz
Nebraska Department of Social
    Services
301 Centennial Mall, South
Lincoln, Nebraska 68509
(402) 471-9206

Ms. Rota Rosaschi
Nevada Department of Human
    Services, Welfare Division
2527 North Carson Street
Carson City, Nevada 89710
(702) 885-3023

Ms. Florence Skantze
New Hampshire Department of
    Health and Welfare
Hazen Drive
Concord, New Hampshire 03301
(603) 271-3602

Ms. Mary Lou Sweeney
New Jersey Department of Youth
and Family Services
1 South Montgomery Street C.N. 719
Trenton, New Jersey 08625
(609) 292-0867

Ms. Regina Jimenez
New Mexico Human Services
Department
PO Box 2348
Santa Fe, New Mexico 87504
(505) 827-4109

Mr. Peter Winkler
New York State Department of Social
Services
40 North Pearl Street
Albany, New York 12243
(518) 473-0855 or 474-2868

Ms. Robin Peacock
N.C. Department of Human Services
Division of Social Services
325 North Salisbury Street
Raleigh, North Carolina 27611
(919) 733-3801

Ms. Virginia Peterson
North Dakota Department of Human
Services
State Capitol Building
Bismarck, North Dakota 58505
(701) 224-3580

Ms. Ann Maxwell
Ohio Department of Human Services
30 East Broad Street, 30th Floor
Columbus, Ohio 43215
(614) 466-8510

Ms. Jane Connor
Oklahoma Department of Human
Services
PO Box 25352
Oklahoma City, Oklahoma 73125
(405) 521-2475

Mr. Fred Stock
Oregon Department of Human
Services
Children's Services Division

198 Commercial Street, SE
Salem, Oregon 97310
(503) 378-4452

Mr. Robert Gioffre
Pennsylvania Department of Public
Welfare
Office of Children, Youth and
Families
PO Box 27653
Harrisburg, Pennsylvania 17105
(717) 787-7556

Ms. Matilda Gonzales Degro
Puerto Rico Department of Social
Services
PO Box 11398
Santurce, Puerto Rico 00910
(809) 723-2127

Mr. John Sinapi
Rhode Island Department of
Children and Their Families
610 Mt. Pleasant Avenue
Providence, Rhode Island 02908
(401) 457-4631

Dr. Kathleen M. Hayes
South Carolina Department of Social
Services
Children and Family Services
PO Box 1520
Columbia, South Carolina 29202-1520
(803) 734-6095

Ms. Patricia Stewart
South Dakota Department of Social
Services
Richard F. Kneip Building
700 Governor's Drive
Pierre, South Dakota 57501
(605) 773-3227

Ms. Joyce N. Harris
Tennessee Department of Human
Services
119-19 Seventh Avenue, North
Nashville, Tennessee 37203
(615) 741-5938

Ms. Susan Klickman
Texas Department of Human
Services

PO Box 2960
Austin, Texas 78769
(512) 450-3302

Ms. Jean D. Womack
Utah Department of Social Services
Office of Community Operations
Salt Lake Central Office
2835 South Main Street
Salt Lake City, Utah 84115
(801) 487-8000

Ms. Maureen Thompson
Vermont Department of Social and
    Rehabilitation Services
103 South Maine Street
Waterbury, Vermont 05676
(802) 241-2150

Ms. Brenda Kerr
Virginia Department of Social
    Services
8007 Discovery Drive
Richmond, Virginia 23229-8699
(804) 281-9081

Ms. Ferrynesia Benjamin
Assistant Director, Social Services
Department of Social Welfare
PO Box 146

Christiansted, St. Croix
Virgin Islands, 00820

Mr. Patrick Weber
Washington Department of Social
    and Health Services
Office Building #2
Olympia, Washington 98504
(206) 753-2178

Ms. Rozella Archer
West Virginia Department of Human
    Services
1900 Washington Street, East
Charleston, West Virginia 25305
(304) 348-7980

Mr. Christopher Marciell
Wisconsin Department of Health and
    Social Services
PO Box 7851
Madison, Wisconsin 53707
(608) 266-0700

Ms. Kay Mathewson
Wyoming Department of Social
    Services
Hathaway Building
Cheyenne, Wyoming 82002
(307) 777-6075

READINGS FOR PROFESSIONALS

Berman, L.C. and Bufferd, R.K. "Family Treatment to Address Loss in Adoptive Families." *Social Casework* 67 (January 1986): 4–12.

Bernstein, J. *Books to Help Children Cope with Separation and Loss.* New York: R.R. Bowker Company, 1977.

Brodzinsky, D.M. "Looking At Adoption Through Rose-Colored Glasses." *Journal of Personality and Social Psychology* 52, 2 (1987): 394–398.

Brodzinsky, D.M.; Shecter, M.E.; and Braff, A.M. "Children's Understanding of Adoption." *Child Development* 55 (1984): 869–878.

Brodzinsky, D.M.; Schecter, M.E.; Braff, A.M.; and Singer, L.M. "Psychological and Academic Adjustment in Adopted Children." *Journal of Consulting and Clinical Psychology* 52 (1984): 582–590.

Clark, E.A., and Hanisee, J. "Intellectual and Adaptive Performance of Asian Children in Adoptive American Settings." *Developmental Psychology* 18 (July 1982): 595–599.

Easson, W. "Special Sexual Problems of the Adopted Adolescent." *Medical Aspects of Human Sexuality* (July 1973): 92–105.

Edelman, R., and Connolly, K. "Psychological Aspects of Infertility." *British Journal of Medical Psychology* 59 (1986): 209–219.

Fales, Mary Jane. *Post-Legal Adoption Services Today.* New York: Child Welfare League of America, 1986.

Feigelman, William, and Silverman, Arnold. "Preferential Adoption: A New Mode of Family Formation." *Social Casework* (1979): 296–305.

———. *Chosen Children: New Patterns of Adoptive Relationships.* New York: Praeger, 1983.

Franklin, David, and Massarik, S. "The Adoption of Children with Medical Conditions." *Child Welfare* XLVIII, 10 (December 1969): 595–560.

Gallagher, Ursula M. "The Adoption of Mentally Retarded Children." *Childen* 15, 1 (January-February 1968): 17–21.

Gill, Owen and Jackson, Barbara. *Adoption and Race: Black, Asian and Mixed Race Children in White Families.* New York: St. Martin's Press, 1983.

Grow, Lucille L., and Shapiro, Deborah. *Transracial Adoption Today: Views of Adoptive Parents and Social Workers.* Washington, DC: Child Welfare League of America, 1986.

Hartman, Ann. *Finding Families: An Ecological Approach to Family Assessment in Adoption.* Beverly Hills: Sage Publications, 1979.

———. *Working with Adoptive Families Beyond Placement.* New York: Child Welfare League of America, 1984.

Hockey, A. "Evaluation of Adoption of the Intellecutally Handicapped: A Retrospective Analysis of 137 Cases." *Journal of Mental Deficiency Research* 24 (September 1980): 187–202.

Hoopes, Janet L. *Prediction in Child Development: A Longitudinal Study of Adoptive and Nonadoptive Families.* New York: Child Welfare League of America, 1982.

Kadushin, Alfred. "Single-Parent Adoptions: An Overview and Some Relevant Research. *Social Service Review* 44 (September, 1970): 263–274.

———. "Child Welfare: Adoption and Foster Care," *Encylopedia of Social Work* (17th issue, Vol. 1). Washington, DC: National Association of Social Workers, 1977, pp. 114–125.

———. "Adopting Older Children: Summary and Implications." In *Early Experience, Myth and Evidence,* edited by A.M. Clarke and A.D.B. Clarke. New York: Free Press, 1977.

Kim, Dong Soo. "Issues in Transracial and Transcultural Adoption." *Social Casework* 59 (October 8, 1978): 477–486.

Kim, S. Peter. *Adoption and Minority Children.* Rockville, MD: NIMH, 1981.

Kim, S. Peter; Hong, Sungdo; and Kim, Bok Soon. "Adoption of Korean Children by New York Area Couples: A Preliminary Study." *Child Welfare* LVIII, 7 (July–August 1979): 419–427.

Kirk, H.D. *Shared Fate: A Theory and Method of Adoptive Relationships* (rev. 1984). Port Angeles, WA: Ben-Simon Publications, 1964.

———. *Adoptive Kinship: A Modern Institution in Need of Reform* (rev. 1985). Port Angeles, WA: Ben Simon Publications, 1981.

Kowal, K., and Schilling, K. "Adoption Through the Eyes of Adult Adoptees." *American Journal of Orthopsychiatry* 55, 3 (1985): 354–561.

Kraft, A.; Palombo, J.; Mitchell, D.; Dean, C.; Meyers, S.; and Schmidt, A.W. "The Psychological Dimensions of Infertility." *American Journal of Orthopsychiatry* 50,4 (October 1980): 618–628.

Ladner, Joyce A. *Mixed Families: Adopting Across Racial Boundaries.* Garden City, NJ: Anchor Press/Doubleday, 1977.

MacFarlane, Kee; Waterman, Jill, et. al. *Sexual Abuse of Young Children: Evaluation and Treatment.* New York: Guilford Press, 1986.

McCoy, J. "Identity as a Factor in the Adoptive Placement of the Older Child." *Child Welfare* XLIX, 1(1961): 14–18.

Meezan, William; Katz, Sanford; and Russo, Eva Manoff. *Adoptions without Agencies: A Study of Independent Adoptions.* New York: Child Welfare League of America, 1978.

Menning, B. *Infertility.* Englewood Cliffs, NJ: Prentice-Hall, 1977.

Miroff, Franklin, and Smith, Jerome. *You're Our Child. A Social-Psychological Approach to Adoption.* Lanham, MD: University Press of America, 1981.

National Committee for Adoption. Adoption Factbook: *U.S. Data, Issues, Regulations and Resources.* Washington, DC: National Committee for Adoption, 1985.

Nelson, K.A. *On the Frontier of Adoption: A Study of Special Needs Adoptive Families.* New York: Child Welfare League of America, 1985.

Sack, Will, and Dale, Diane. "Abuse and Deprivation in Failing Adoptions." *Child Abuse and Neglect* 64 (1982): 443–451.

Sants, H. "Genealogical Bewilderment in Children with Substitute Parents." *Child Adoption* 47 (1965): 32–42.

Schwartz, L.L. "Adoption Custody and Family Therapy." *American Journal of Family Therapy* 12, 4 (1984): 51–58.

Shireman, Joan F. and Johnson, Penny R. "Single Persons as Adoptive Parents." *Social Service Review* 50, 1 (March 1976): 103–116.

Silin, Marilyn. "Why Many Placed Children Have Learning Difficulties." *Child Welfare* XLII, 8 (1963): 345–352.

Smith, Dorothy W., and Sherwen, Laurie Nehls. *Mothers and Their Adopted Children.* New York: The Tiresias Press, Inc., 1983.

Sorosky, A.D.; Baran, A.; and Pannor, R. *The Adoption Triangle: Sealed or Open Records: How They Affect Adoptees, Birth Parents and Adoptive Parents.* New York: Anchor Press/Doubleday, 1984.

Stein, Leslie, and Hoopes, Janet. *Identity Formation in the Adopted Adolescent.* New York: Child Welfare League of America, 1985.

Taichert, L.C., and Harvin, D.D. "Adoption and Children with Learning and Behavior Problems." *The Western Journal of Medicine* 122 (1975): 464–470.

Ward, Margaret. "Parental Bonding in Older Child Adoptions." *Child Welfare* LX, 1 (January 1981): 24–33.

Watson, J. "Bibliotherapy for Abused Children." *School Counselor* 27 (1980): 204–209.

Wieder, H. "The Family Romance Fantasies of Adopted Children." *Psychoanalytic Quarterly* 46, 2 (1977): 185–200.

READINGS FOR ADOPTIVE PARENTS

Bolles, E. *The Penguin Adoption Book.* New York: Penguin Books, 1984.

Burgess, Linda. *The Art of Adoption.* New York: Norton, 1981.

Gilman, L. *The Adoption Resource Book.* New York: Harper and Row, 1984.

Grabe, Pam, and Schreiber, Carolyn. *A Common Sense Approach to Therapy Options for Families.* (Order from Mental Health Association in Butler County, 127 E Wayne Street, Butler, PA 16001.)

Jewett, C. *Helping Children Cope with Separation and Loss.* Cambridge, MA: Harvard Common Press, 1982.

————. *Adopting the Older Child*. Cambridge, MA: Harvard Common Press, 1978.

Menning, B. *Infertility*. Englewood Cliffs, NJ: Prentice- Hall, 1977.

Lifton, B.J. *Lost and Found*. New York: Bantam Books, 1981.

Miroff, Franklin, and Smith, Jerome. *You're Our Child. A Social-Psychological Approach to Adoption*. Lanham, MD: University Press of America, 1981.

Smith, D., and Sherwen, L. *Mothers and Their Adopted Children*. New York: The Tiresias Press, 1983.

APPENDICES

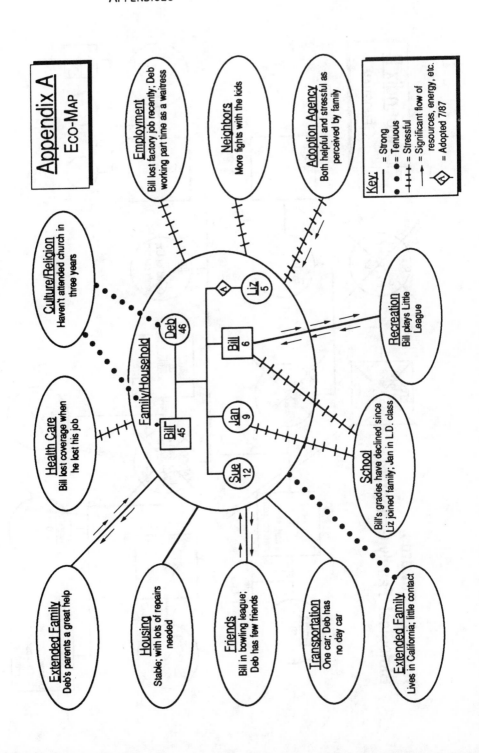

Appendix A
ECO-MAP

Employment
Bill lost factory job recently; Deb working part time as a waitress

Neighbors
More fights with the kids

Adoption Agency
Both helpful and stressful as perceived by family

Culture/Religion
Haven't attended church in three years

Health Care
Bill lost coverage when he lost his job

Extended Family
Deb's parents a great help

Housing
Stable; with lots of repairs needed

Friends
Bill in bowling league; Deb has few friends

Transportation
One car; Deb has no day car

Extended Family
Lives in California; little contact

School
Bill's grades have declined since Liz joined family; Jan in L.D. class

Recreation
Bill plays Little League

Family/Household

Sue 12 · Jan 9 · Bill 6 · Liz 5
Bill 45 · Deb 46

Key:
_____ = Strong
• • • • • = Tenuous
++++++ = Stressful
———→ = Significant flow of resources, energy, etc.
⬦A = Adopted 7/87

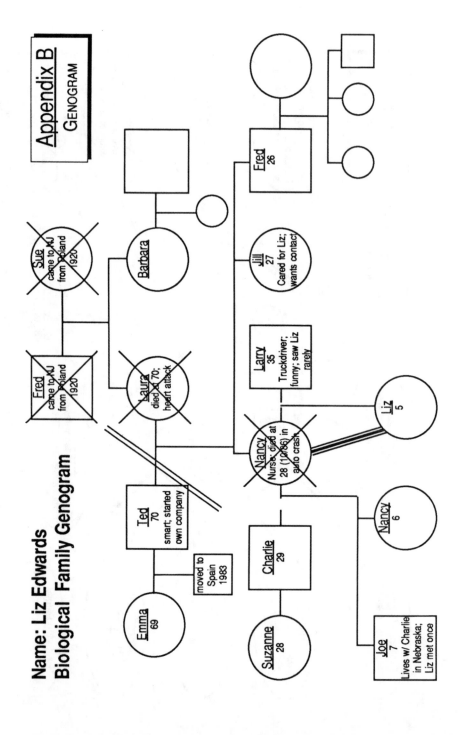

Name: Liz Edwards
Biological Family Genogram

Appendix B
GENOGRAM

Name: Liz Edwards
Adoptive Family Genogram

Key:
○ = female
□ = male
 = strong bond
⊠ = deceased
 = immed. family
 = cut off
◇A = adopted
— — = household unit

REFERENCES

Anderson, J. "Grief Issues in Counseling Adoptive Families." In *Adoption Resources for Mental Health Professionals*, edited by P. Grabe and P. Reitnauer. Butler, PA: The Mental Health Association in Butler County, 1986.

Barth, R.P.; Berry, M.; Carson, M.; Goodfield, R.; and Feinberg, B. "Contributors to Disruption and Dissolution of Older Child Adoptions." *Child Welfare* LXV, 4 (July–August 1986): 359–371.

Berman, L., and Bufferd, R. "Family Treatment to Address Loss in Adoptive Families." *Social Casework* 67, 1 (January 1986): 4–12.

Bowen, M. *Family Therapy in Clinical Practice*, New York: Aronson, 1978.

Brandt., A. "Bloodlines." *Esquire* (September 1984): 21–22.

Brodzinsky, D. "Looking at Adoption Through Rose-Colored Classes." *Journal of Personality and Social Psychology* 52, 2 (1987): 394–398.

Churchill, S.; Carlson, B.; and Nybell, L. *No Child Is Unadoptable*. Beverly Hills, CA: Sage Publications, 1979.

Erikson, E. *Identity: Youth and Crisis*. New York: W.W. Norton, 1968.

Fahlberg, V. *Attachment and Separation*. Lansing, MI: Michigan Department of Social Services, 1979.

Fales, M.J. *Post-Legal Adoption Services Today*. New York: Child Welfare League of America, Inc., 1986.

Feigelman, W., and Silverman, A. *Chosen Children: New Patterns of Adoptive Relationships*. New York: Praeger, 1983.

Frey, L. *Preserving Permanence*. Boston, MA: Project IMPACT, Inc., 1986.

Frisk, M. "Identity Problems and Confused Conceptions of the Genetic Ego in Adopted Children During Adolescence." *Acta Paedo Psychiatrica* 31 (1964): 6–12.

Hartman, A. *Working with Adoptive Families Beyond Placement*. New York: Child Welfare League of America, 1984.

Hughes, R., and Rycus, J. *Child Welfare Services for Children with Developmental Disabilities*. New York: Child Welfare League of America, 1983.

Jewett, C. *Adopting the Older Child*. Boston, MA: The Harvard Common Press, 1978.

Kadushin, A. *Adopting Older Children*. New York: Columbia University Press, 1970.

Kagan, R., and Reid, W. "Critical Factors in the Adoption of Emotionally Disturbed Youths. *Child Welfare* LXV, 1 (January-February 1986): 63–73.

Kennel, J., Voos, D.; and Klaus, M. "Parent-Infant Bonding." In *Child Abuse and Neglect*, edited by R. Helfer and C. Kempe. Cambridge, MA: Ballinger Publishing Co., 1976.

Kirk, H.D. *Shared Fate: A Theory and Method of Adoptive Relationships* (rev. 1984). Port Angeles, WA: Ben Simon Publications, 1964.

––––––. *Adoptive Kinship: A Modern Institution in Need of Reform* (rev. 1985). Port Angeles, WA: Ben Simon Publications, 1981.

Kraft, A.: Palombo, J.; Mitchell, D.; Dean, C.; Meyers, S.; and Schmidt, A.W. "Psychological Dimensions of Infertility." *American Journal of Orthopsychiatry* 50,4 (October 1980): 618–628.

Levine, M. "The Child with Learning Disabilities." In *The Practical Management of the Developmentally Disabled Child*. St. Louis, MO: C.V. Moseby Co., 1980.

National Committee for Adoption. *Adoption Factbook: U.S. Data, Issues, Regulations, and Resources*. Washington, DC: National Committee for Adoption, 1985.

Nelson, K.A. *On the Frontier of Adoption: A Study of Special Needs Adoptive Families*. New York: Child Welfare League of America, Inc., 1985.

Reitnauer, P., and Grabe, P. *Focusing Training for Mental Health Professionals on Issues of Foster Care and Adoption*. Butler, PA: The Mental Health Association in Butler County, 1985.

Satir, V. *Conjoint Family Therapy*. Palo Alto, CA: Science and Behavior Books, 1967.

Smith, D., and Sherwen, L. *Mothers and Their Adopted Children*. New York: The Tiresias Press, Inc., 1983.